REPURPOSE

matt arbuckle
peter atkins
chris carmody
nicole ellis
erwin fabian
robert motherwell
elizabeth newman
trish roan

ANU DRILL HALL GALLERY
11 NOVEMBER - 18 DECEMBER 2016

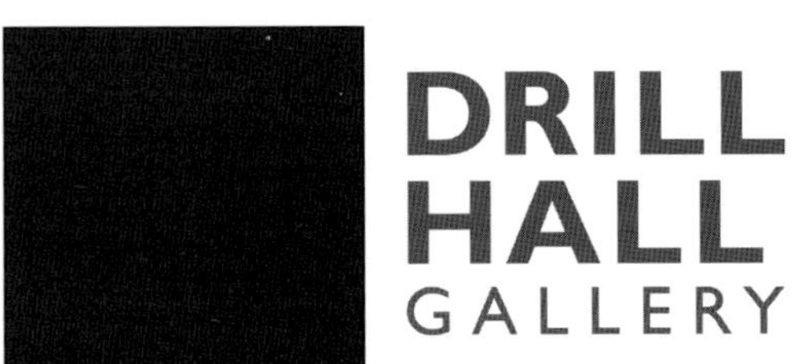

Chris Carmody, *Yellow Box 1.2*, 2016 (cat no 19)

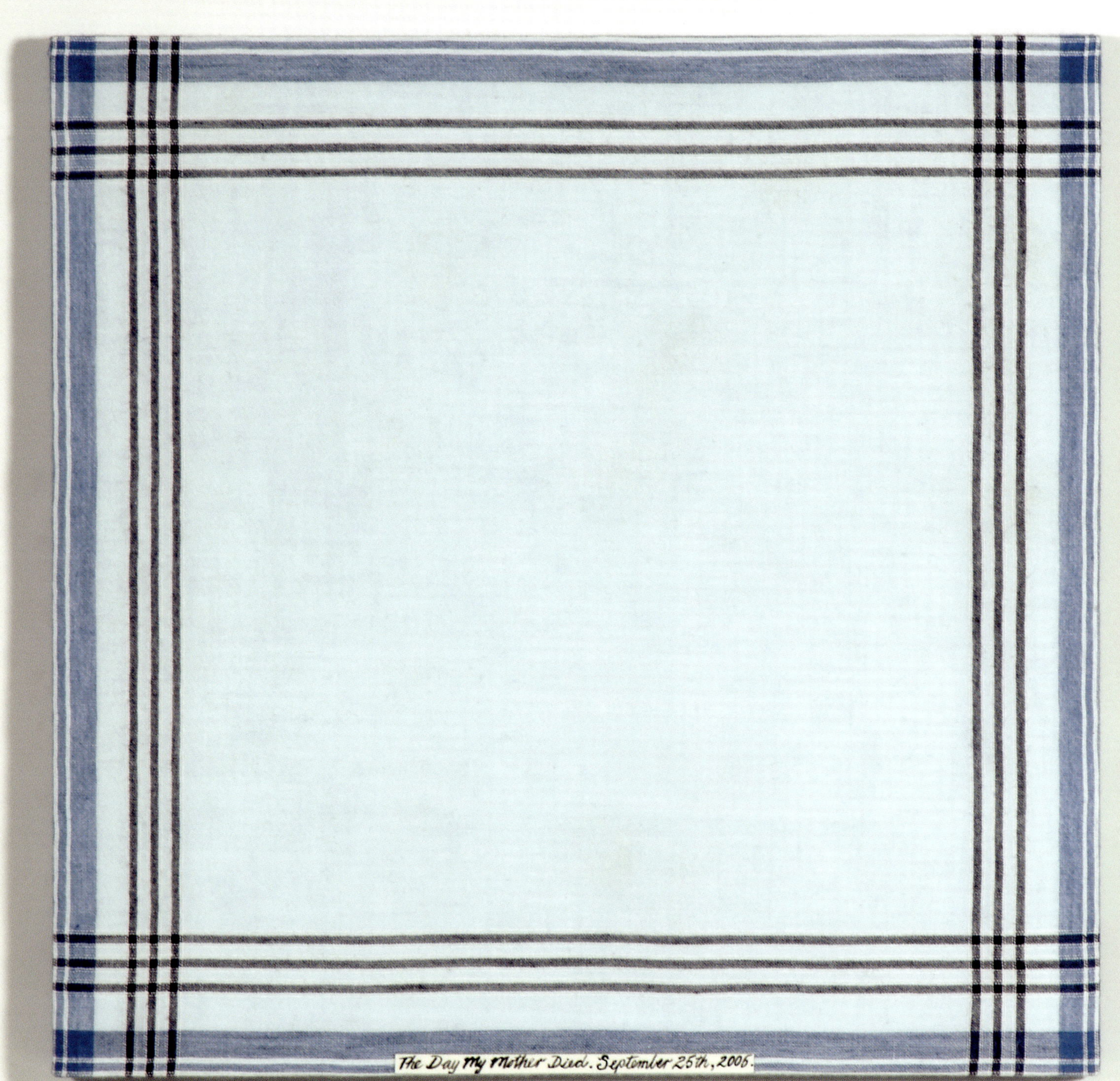
The Day My Mother Died. September 25th, 2006.

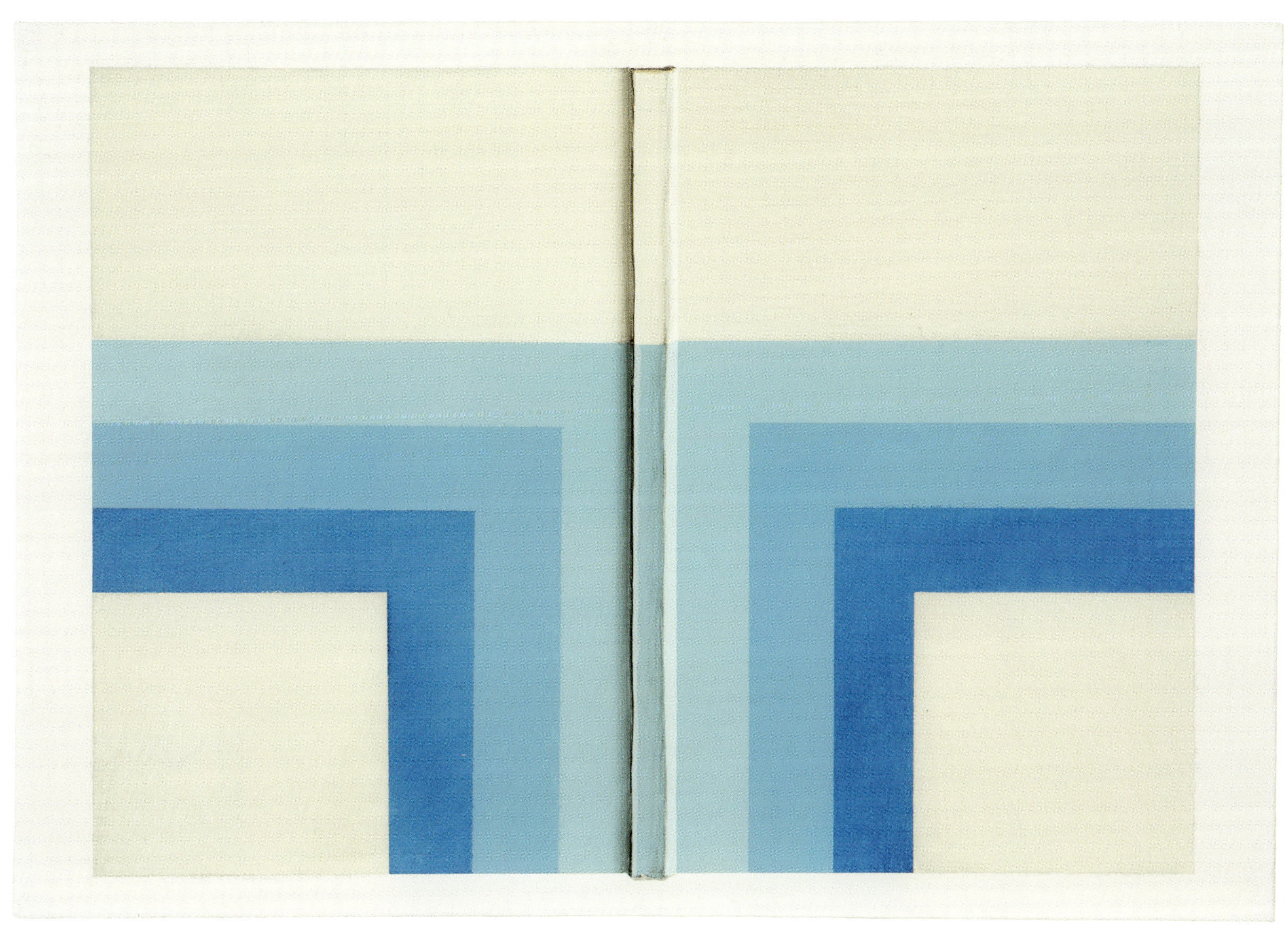

above: Chris Carmody, *803 ABR*, 2016 (cat no 17); opposite: Peter Atkins, *Brunswick Journal,* 2005 detail (cat no 5)

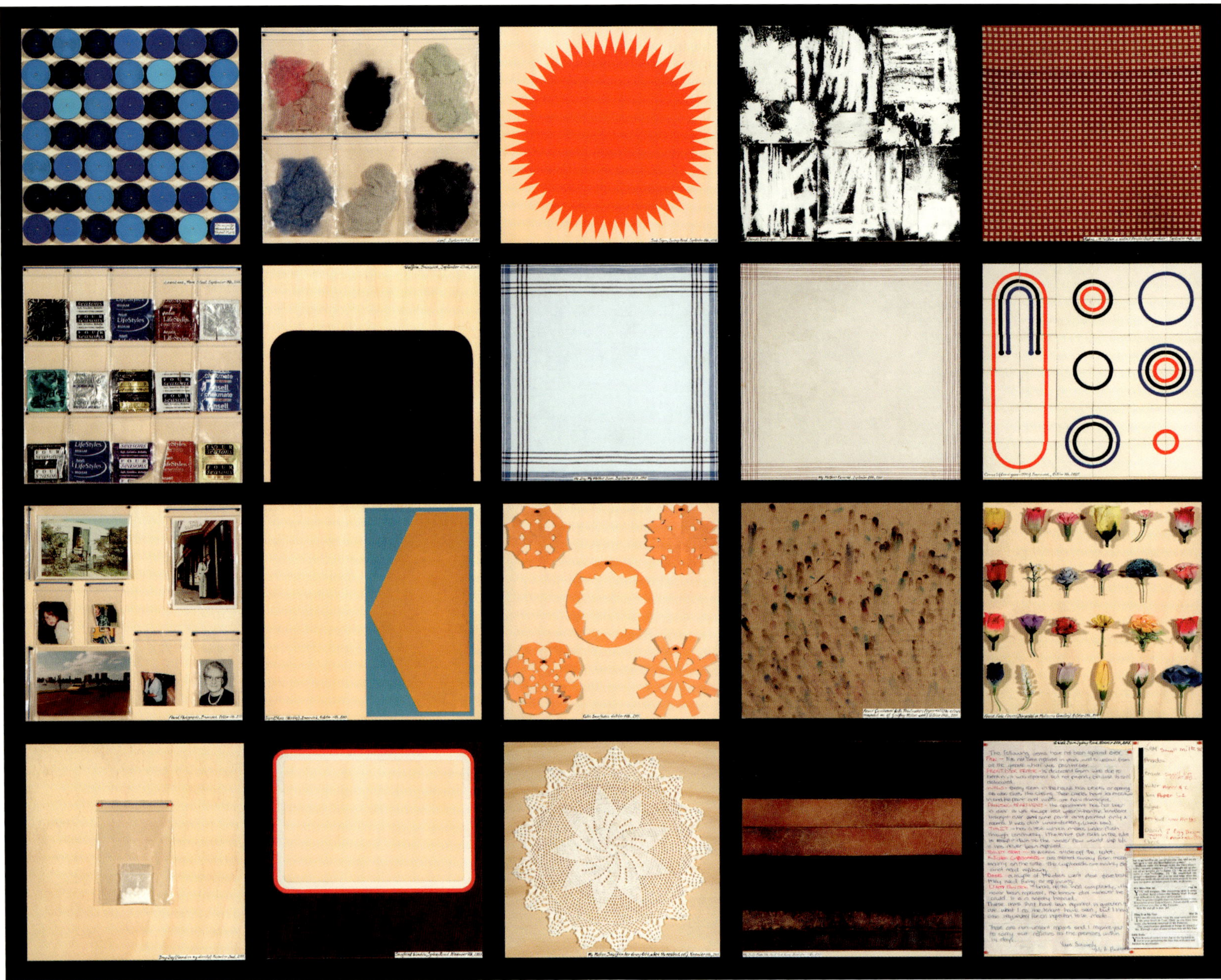

above: Peter Atkins, *Brunswick Journal,* 2005 (cat no 5); opposite: *The Bix Beiderbecke Legend,* 2013 (cat no 8)

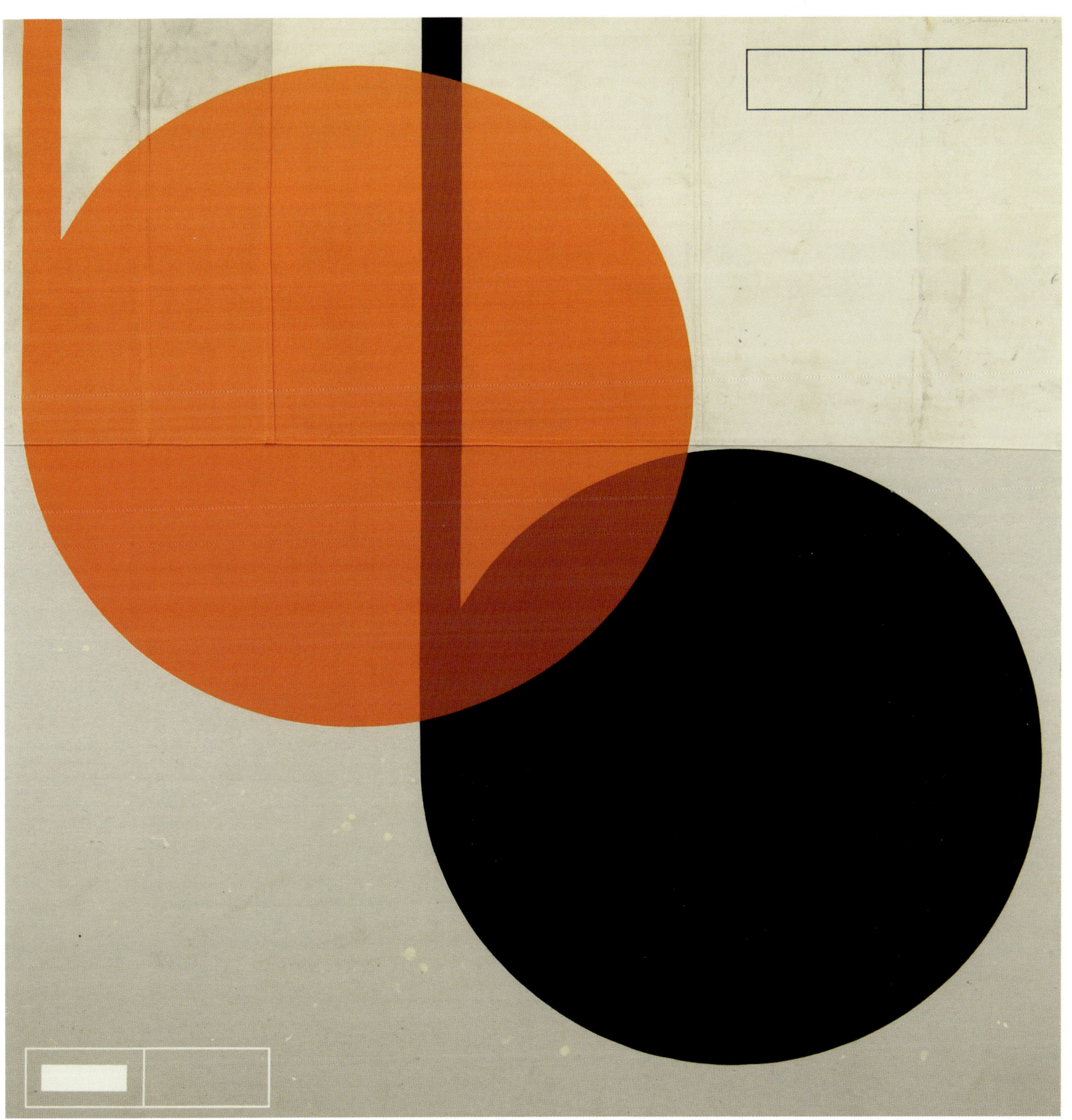

Trish Roan, *Star Map,* 2014 (cat no 53)

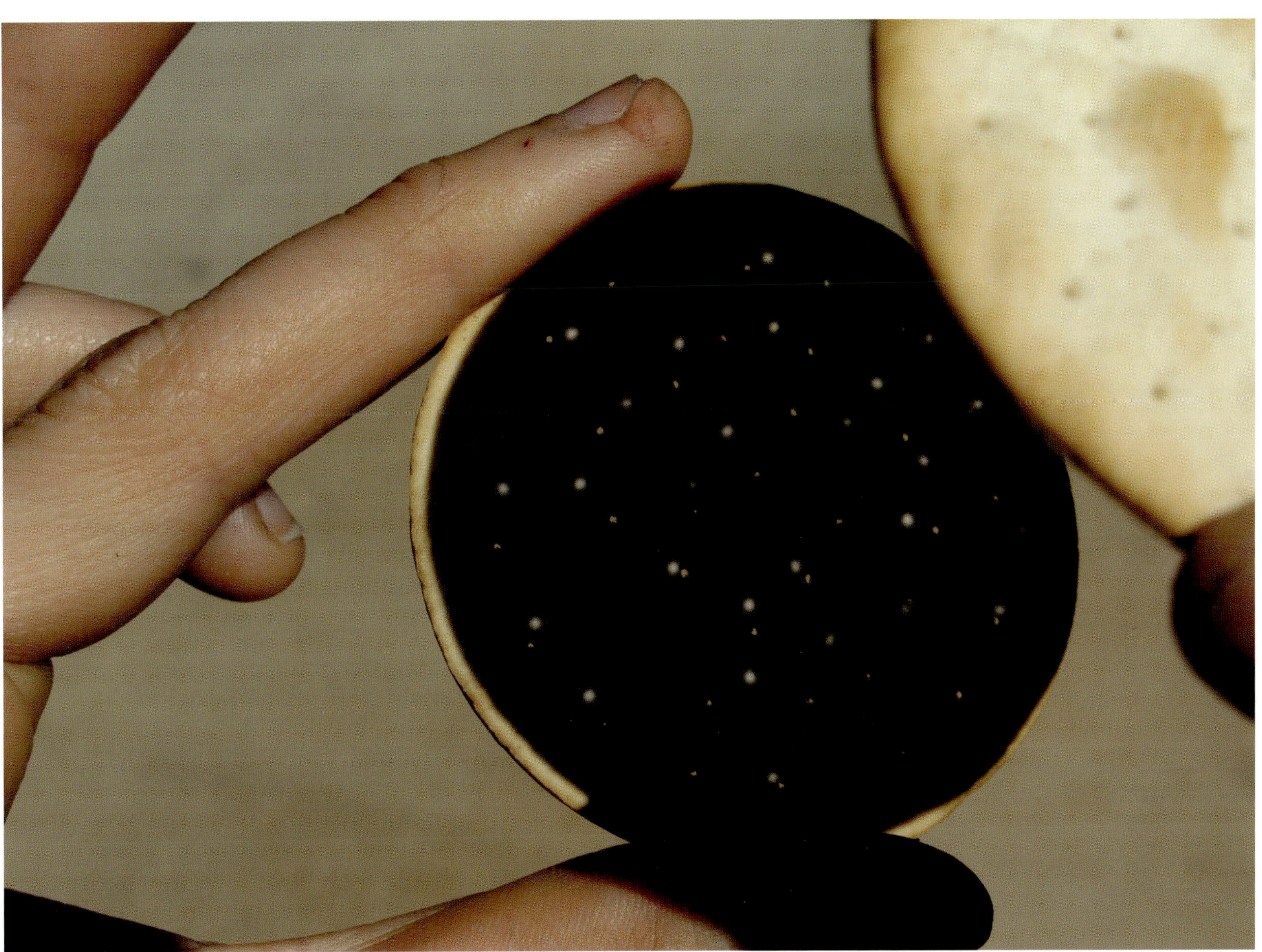

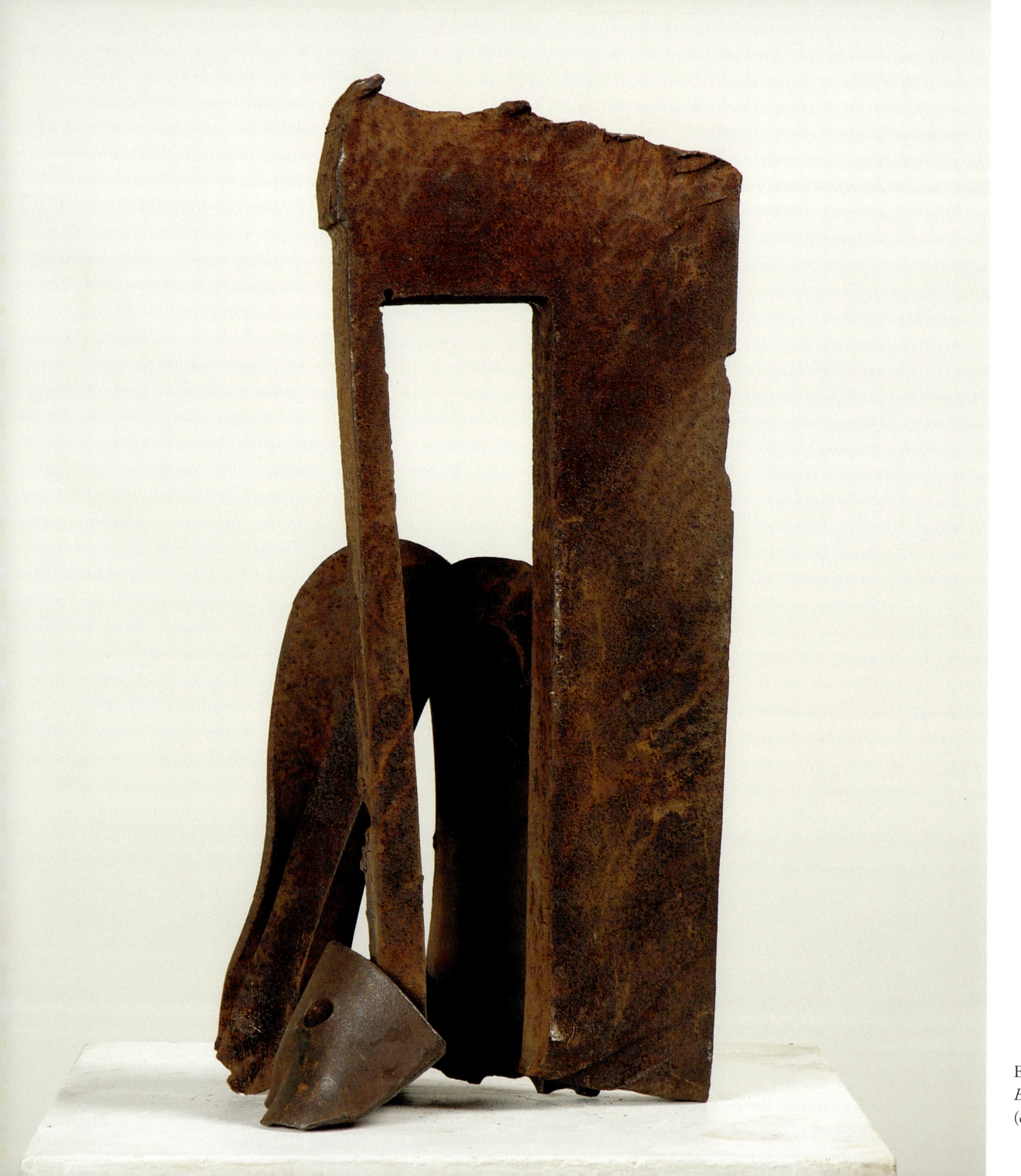

Erwin Fabian,
Exit, 2008
(cat no 32)

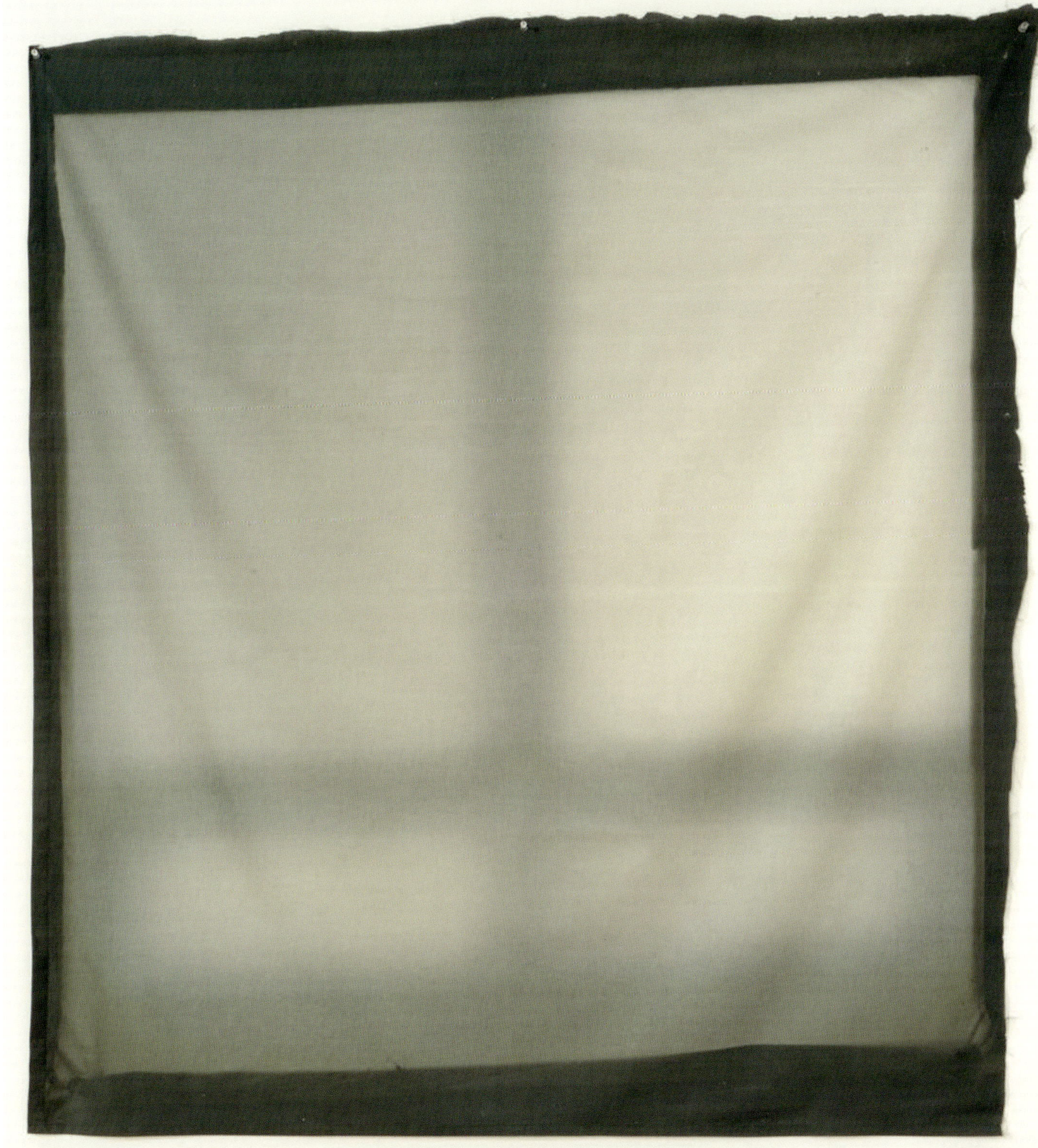

Chris Carmody,
Inner North, 2013
(cat no 10)

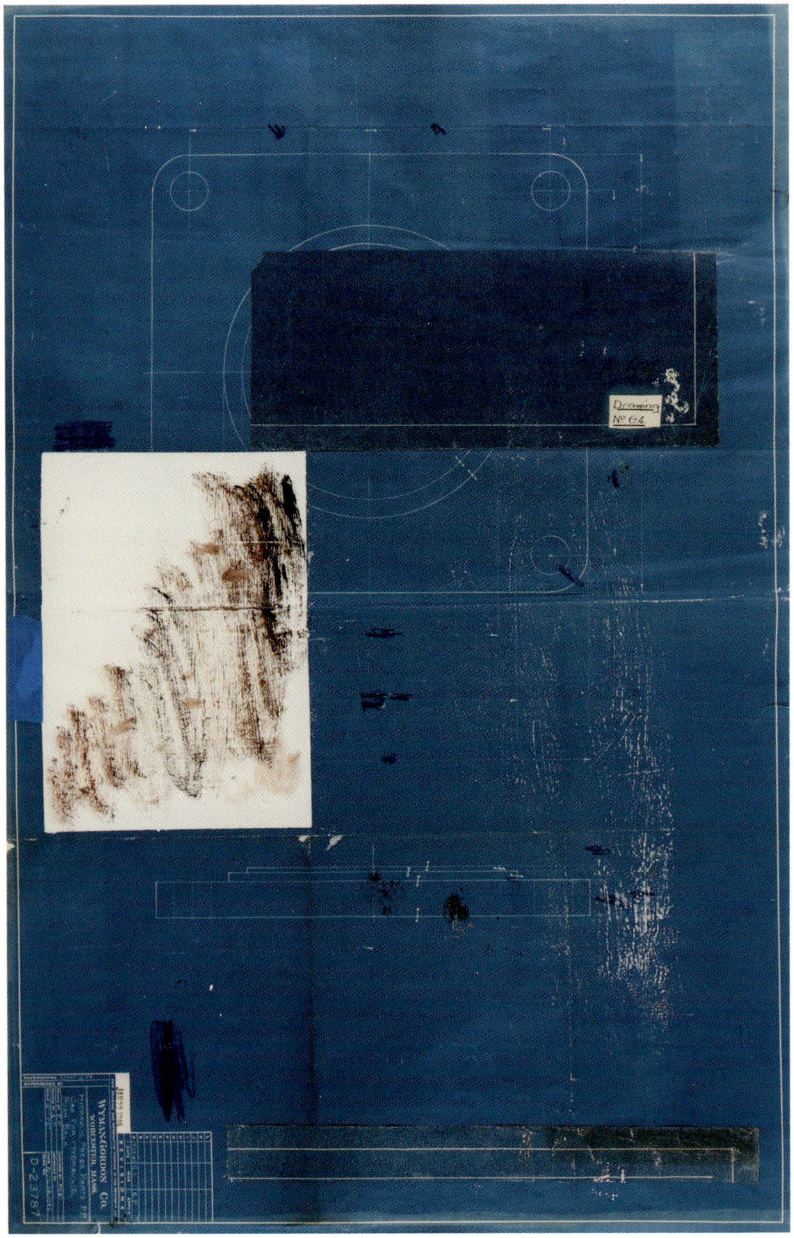

Drawing
Nº 64

WYMAN-GORDON CO.
WORCESTER, MASS.
D-23787

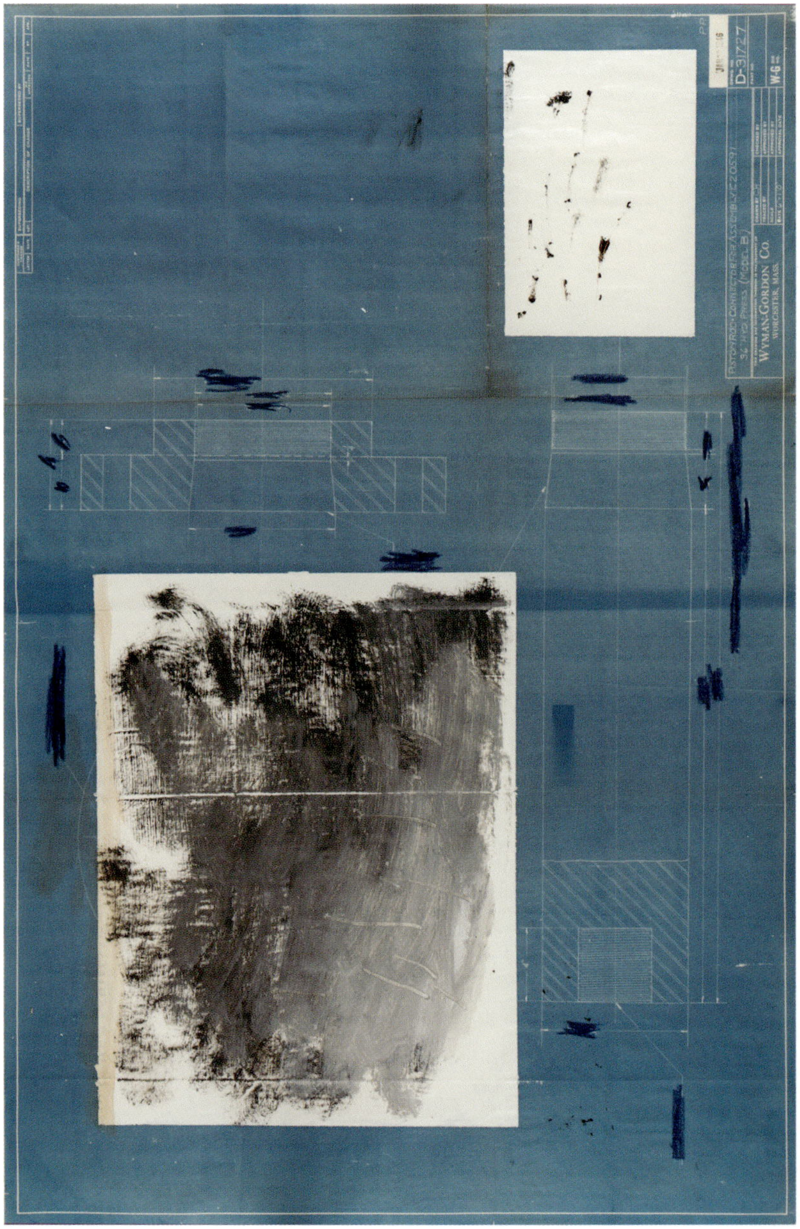

D-31727
W-G
WYMAN-GORDON CO.
WORCESTER, MASS.

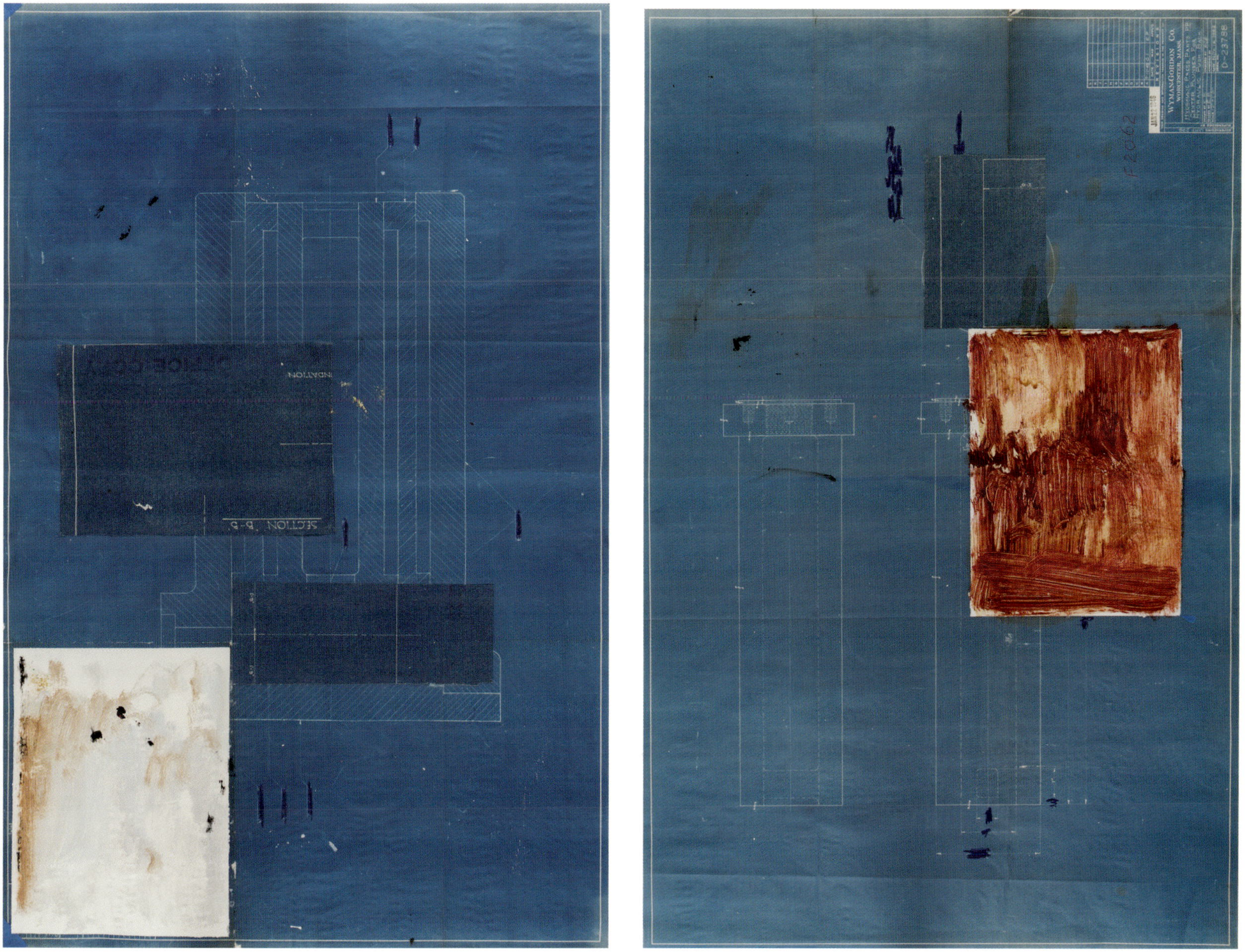

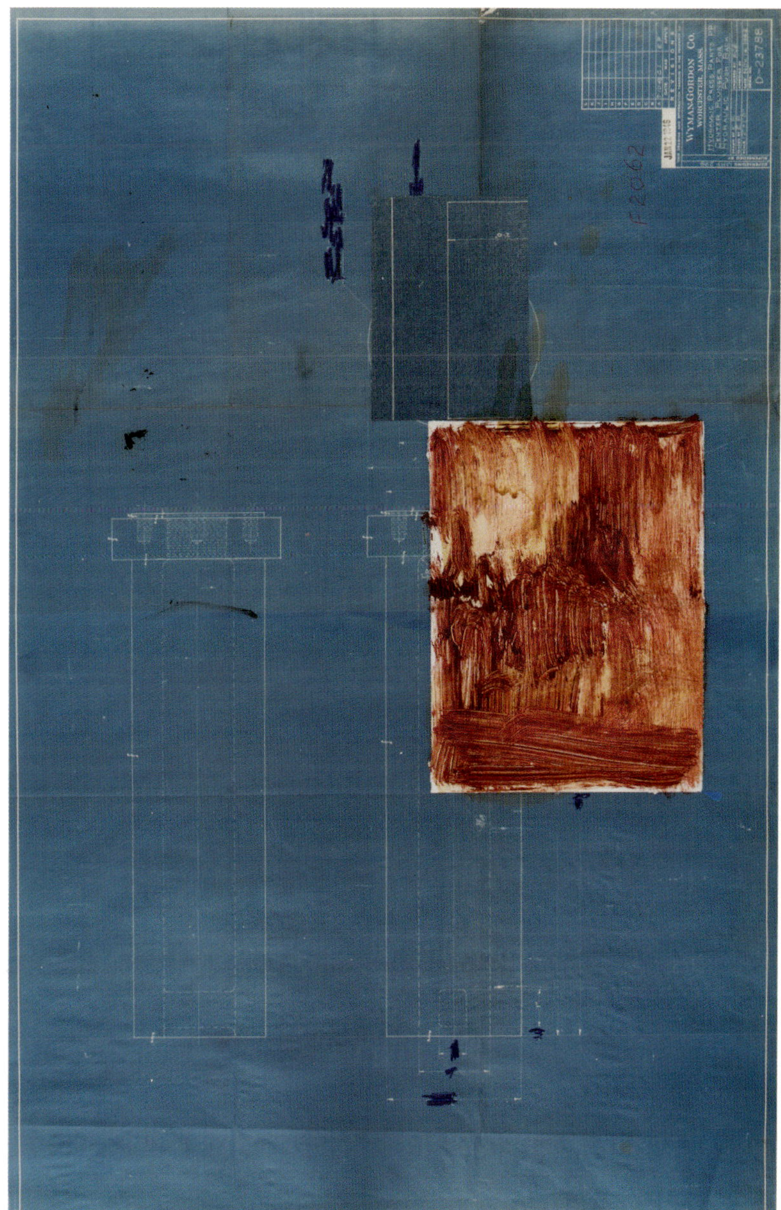

Matt Arbuckle, *Sliding Door Opportunity*, 2016 (cat no 4)

Naturally I began my artistic education 'with a model.' I had learnt to paint from nature and when I was convinced that I had to free myself from the model, it was a rather hard task … I forced myself, and the liberation was achieved by intuitive impulses that widened the gap between me and my model. At such moments one harkens to an inner voice, oblivious of what it will lead to. That is what I call adventure. – Georges Braque[1]

Greek art had a purely human conception of beauty. It took man as the measure of perfection. The art of the new painters takes the infinite universe as the ideal
- Guillaume Apollinaire[2]

Leading into the twentieth century, physicists, astronomers and thinkers 'perceived that certain phenomena could no longer be explained, that they were, so to speak, inconceivable, in short, that they themselves could no longer grasp them and namely, *represent* them… Everything was once again in question.'[3] The admission of the limitless extent of the universe and other conundrums – the proposition of a fourth dimension by thinkers such as Henri Bergson – put into doubt the very possibility of human comprehension. 'Everything was once again in question!' How does one approach representing a world that has been predicated on a false understanding? How does one confront the inconceivable? These questions struck at the very core of a rationalised existence.

If traditional humanist ways of understanding were shaken, the possibilities for reorienting and replacing them were magnified in compensation. Bergson celebrated the evolutionary unfolding of human creative resources, elevating the role of intuition, the imagination and the appreciation of vitality (*élan vital*) as a superlative source of discovery. The mind-expanding implications for renewed creativity within an as yet uncharted cognitive milieu appealed as powerfully to artists as to scientists and metaphysicians. For visual artists, many of whom learnt of these matters by hearsay (at second or third hand), Bergson's postulation exposed a fallibility in the link between subject and object, a relationship long supposed to be straightforward in the Western tradition. From now on, the subject-object relation was characterised as an indeterminate state in which flux was the essential condition. These ideas may have chimed in with intimations that had already been broached in the experimental painting of the Impressionists, and in particular Cézanne.

In certain linguistic speculations, structuralist thinkers such as Ferdinand de Saussure recognised the inherent frailty of existing theories.[4] Beholding the arbitrariness of the sign, they threw into question the relationship between signifier and its referent (famously 'bracketing the referent'). The Symbolist poets, Rimbaud, Baudelaire and Mallarmé, equally, revelled in the non-transparency and malleability of language, embracing slippages, uncertainty, and multiple meanings to emphasise the materiality of text, the musicality of prosody and the plasticity of syntax. For the Symbolists, reading was conceived as an associative, intuitive, open-ended kind of wonderment.

Within these linguistic and literary circles, the knowability of the world as revealed by our senses came under interrogation. Objects, once considered the stable currency of truth, became doubtful phenomena. As the privileged signifiers of common experience, they now belonged less certainly to the material world than to the mind of the beholder.

The basis of art in representation underwent a related crisis of confidence. Some artists were afflicted by doubts that were ontological, epistemological, technical and formal. Although these same artists tended to be treated by their peers as carriers of a dreaded disease, their condition of doubt nonetheless became defining of Modernity.[5]

The Post-Impressionist painters mapped out several possible directions. Negations of naturalism took various forms: one trajectory led to non-objectivity; another dramatized simultaneous, multiple, clashing points of view and discordant pictorial codes; a third resorted to schematised ideograms suspended within a hermetic utopia. 'Modern art' emerged from this crisis of representation.

For the purposes of the current exhibition, our most significant flashpoint occurs around 1910, when Picasso and Braque dispensed with the need for a model, relinquishing their dependency on a pre-existing motif. For the two young artists, traditional aspects of *mimesis* – copying and transliterating the world as it appeared – were deemed facile and illusory, insufficient to address changing conceptions of space and time. Rejecting mimetic conventions, Picasso and Braque exploded Euclidian geometry and proposed new ciphers for the multi-faceted vitality of experience.

Their conjurations of fractured lines and mottled, crystalline planes generated abstract configurations which might or might not have been qualified with details identifying these compositions as figures, landscapes or still lifes. There were several notable metamorphoses at this time where figure compositions became still lifes or vice versa.

As if to draw attention to the absence of a model, Braque and Picasso introduced found elements into their work. In 1912 they pasted sections of wood grain wallpaper or swatches of newsprint on the surface of their drawings. Initially these *papiers collés* may not have been conceived as self-sufficient works, but as preparatory studies destined to be converted into paintings. Yet the *papiers collés* proved legitimate, vital works of art in their own right; the found objects enriched the abstractness of the Cubist premise, establishing a dialectical rapport with the 'real' world. A spectator can clearly identify the 'foreign' element as wallpaper, for example, and be guided by its material association to infer a table or guitar, and also read a spatial configuration into overlapping lines and planes. In effect, the found object functions as a substitute 'model' extracted straight out of the quotidian world. What, if anything, could sabotage the illusion of a transparent picture plane more effectively than the inclusion of these chunks of unprocessed reality?

One of the perennial anxieties of theorists and artists is the fear of entropy. The second law of thermodynamics implies that all matter and energy tend to degenerate into a state of inert uniformity which only chaos can redeem. The law of thermodynamics forms a sort of parallel to Hegelian dialectics where the interplay of thesis and antithesis, force and counter-force generates dynamism. However, when the tension of opposition expires, entropy prevails. For Modernist innovators, the restaged clash of form and content, real and ideal, presentation and re-presentation, generated by the inclusion of collaged objects served to revive the stalemate of pure abstraction, reviving the possibility of dialectical progress. The foreign element became a stand-in for the model that had gone missing.

Repurpose takes its impetus from the revelation of Cubist collage and the re-positioning of the found object to act as signifier and spark a catalytic chain of events. Separated by several generations from the founders of Cubism, the artists in this exhibition – Matt Arbuckle, Peter Atkins, Chris Carmody, Nicole Ellis, Erwin Fabian, Robert Motherwell, Elizabeth Newman and Trish Roan – are clearly much less preoccupied with representation than were the Cubists. Nonetheless, their artwork results from similar motivations, revelling in a subtle, sceptical appreciation of the conundrums of time and space, staging a distancing and disentanglement of stimuli derived from their physical environment.

In 1935 Picasso told Christian Zervos: 'There is no abstract art. You must always start with something. Afterwards you can remove all traces of reality. There's no danger then anyway, because the idea of the object will have left an indelible mark.'[6] When asked by Georges Charbonnier in the 1950s if the object was his subject in painting, Georges Braque responded:

'No. I believe that colours and forms come into play before all else. I think that poetic art – if I may use the expression – consists of giving life to those forms and colours, in other words: out of a white patch on the canvas, making a towel. But I believe that the white patch is a thing conceived before the knowledge of what it will become. So there is a transformation of the thing. You could say: a poetic transformation of the thing.'[7]

...

What is the most vital moment of realisation – of *creation* – held in common by all these artists? Within objects, found materials and discarded substances there lies an invitation to create, to perform a poetic transformation. In this regard, Peter Atkins can speak for his peers and predecessors: 'I am totally directed by found materials and I am constantly surprised by the possibilities they present,' he says.[8]

Atkins' practice consists of collecting, cataloguing, analysing and synthesising objects that, for him, convey an irresistible aesthetic fascination and emotive charge. The artist sees his *Journal* series (see illus. p. 4 & 6) as an experiential recording of his environment, binding together the most disparate found materials to develop episodes vivified by memory. Memory is 'just the intersection of mind and matter,'[9] stated Henri Bergson. From this Bertrand Russell extrapolated that 'things remembered survive in memory, and thus interpenetrate present things: past and present are not mutually external but are mingled in the unity of consciousness.'[10] Hence time does not function in a linear direction, but can be refracted by the multiplicity of association and the richness of felt immediacy to precipitate a *creative realisation*.

The spectator of Atkins' *Journal* must correlate a plurality of cross-references, deducing hypothetical connections. The human imagination spontaneously strives to determine an order, even one that is not possible to verify or which cannot be precisely fixed.

In contrast to the dispersal of attention in the *Journal* series, Atkins' large paintings (see *The Bix Beiderbecke Legend*, 2013, illus. p. 7) are commandingly single and static in focus. The pretext here is a found object which is an already sophisticated graphic construct. The record covers of the 1950s and 60s were created by graphic designers steeped in the Bauhaus aesthetic. Atkins effects a purification of their designs and reveals the elegant, striking, timelessly stylish abstract underpinnings. It is the informational content (the names, titles, typography, logos, photographic inserts) that Atkins purges and the compositional essence that he foregrounds.

In his essay *Entropy and Art,* Rudolf Arnheim notes that 'tension reduction is achieved when, in interest of orderliness, superfluous components are eliminated from a system and needed ones supplied.'[11] However it is important to note that in Peter Atkins' case tensions are by no means abolished. In the *EP Project* (illus. p. 34 & 35) there is the discreet application of collaged elements, causing a subtle effect of fragmentation, in that the collage does not entirely support the imperatives of the graphic template. The gritty materiality of the support is affirmed in opposition to the hard-edged smoothness of the graphic configuration. By reducing the complexity of formal relationships and carefully moderating the competing claims of a slightly discordant materiality, Atkins retains a productive dialectical tension.

The pre-existence of a chosen object acts as a poetic source for Chris Carmody's recent series of paintings, where books provide the model (see illus. p. 5 & 37). A quotation that the artist is particularly fond of comes from Boswell's biography of Samuel Johnson:

'Knowledge is of two kinds. We know a subject ourselves, or we know where we can find information upon it. When we enquire into any subject, the first thing we have to do is to know what books have treated of it. This leads us to look at catalogues, and at the backs of books in libraries.'[12]

It may be claimed that the whole history of human thought is contained within the pages of books – yet, as Dr Johnson implies, there are things we know best 'in themselves,' through empirical experience. Carmody's paintings highlight this discrepancy by contradicting the solidity of the book with the fleeting, vaporous qualities of light. Carmody's subjects have been selected from various libraries where they have been shelved in some instances for decades, coexisting all this time with their neighbouring titles. Shafts of light beaming onto the stacks effect a slow degradation: the books begin to fade. The profile of one book may act as a shield to its neighbour, masking out the light to imprint an echo of its form on the opposing cover. The books have been catalogued, arranged and codified before they were encountered by the artist – subjected to particular administrative, physical and temporal circumstances which define their appearance and ultimately recommend them as pretexts for Carmody's paintings. As he says:

'There is a relationship between the books and the paintings as objects, which has been mediated through my sight and hands, with the measured application of line and edges soft and hard, colours and other things. A canvas is stretched to resemble the proportions of a particular book, at an exact scale. But the painting can only be exactly itself.'[13]

Carmody's paintings hinge on the dualism of their subjects: the ambivalence of presence and absence, objectness and immateriality, mathematical certainty and intuition, presentation and representation. They make visible a durational act: in *Creative Evolution*, Bergson noted that 'form is only a snapshot view of transition.'[14] As a foil to the dreamy, metaphysical, abstract qualities of Carmody's paintings, the tokens of representation – the *trompe-l'œil* book spine, call numbers, areas of removed tape and the publication details – jolt the spectator back to a world of hard facts. A cyclical loop ensues, recalling Bergson's epoch-making vision: 'We see the material world melt back into a single flux.'[15] Indeed, the paradoxes of Carmody's art align his paintings almost perfectly with Bergson's characterisation of an 'image':

'By image we mean a certain existence which is more than that which the idealist calls a *representation*, but less than that which the realist calls a *thing*, – an existence placed halfway between the "thing" and the representation.'[16]

Carmody intentionally plays on the viewer's knowledge of modern abstraction, collapsing the abstractionists' evocation of sublimity (a metaphor for creative force) with the evocation of the destructive powers of light. He is aware of the fact that, during its long history, the discourse on the sublime has been fixated on events of light – sunrise, sunset, the rainbow, lightning, moonlight. Carmody's paintings attest to the transformative power of light, and perhaps nothing among his works evokes the sublime as potently as *Inner North* (illus. p. 11). As Apollinaire wrote in *The Cubist Painters: Aesthetic Meditations*: 'All bodies are equal before the light and their modifications result from the luminous power that constructs at its whim.'[17]

For Apollinaire it was light whose vibrations activated the musical instruments in Braque's paintings, although 'it is Saint Cecilia herself who makes his instruments sound.'[18] Here Apollinaire looked to Mallarmé's poem *Sainte Cecilia* (1865) where an old viola sits faded beneath a stained-glass window. Light streaming through the glass and the apparition of Saint Cecilia, her wings forming a harp, stimulates the instrument to produce music from the void.[19] The poem infers that a virtual musicality exists within the instrument. Within its void is a latency awaiting imminent manifestation.

In Picasso and Braque's collages this metaphorical aptitude, the ability to be activated and become awakened to participate, was of central concern. The form of the guitar or mandolin was completely mutable and could alter into a cipher for a head, a woman's body, or a womb pregnant with thought.[20] *Papiers collés* such as Picasso's *Guitar, sheet music and wine glass* (1912) or his *Guitar* constructions (1912) are centred around a potent empty space, '*au creux néant musicien*' (whose hollow nothingness is musical). From the condensed void a note forms, resonates and proceeds to engulf the space that surrounds it.

Like Picasso's *Guitar, sheet music and wine glass*, Elizabeth Newman's collages (illus. p 32 & 48) pivot around reversals of positive and negative, affirming the plasticity of space and the ambiguous character of the void. 'I like to bring "the nothing" into being for some reason. Making a cut, finding a hole; pointing to a void,' she says.[21] Newman's art emphasises an inherent division in her subjects – of inside and outside, object and image: a wood-grain monolith becomes porous, shedding its mass; a breathing volume devours space while simultaneously radiating it back into the world; an object corresponds to the breadth of its possibility. As the poet Francis Ponge wrote:

'Only here can we see how, in the void, things are made and unmade, how they are born and die and are reborn different, by the permutation of their elements. And so we see the whole, where nothing is ever created out of nothing.'[22]

For these artists the void might be synonymous with Bergson's fourth dimension: the realm of imagination, its infinite reach offering the freedom to construct at one's whim.[23] Newman's found object, *Untitled* (illus. p. 31), not only focuses on the void as a gateway – open to anything and everything beyond it – but may also function symbolically, denoting the creative evolution of something out of nothing. 'For me' Newman says, 'art-making is an expression and manifestation of the artist's subjectivity. It is some Thing of the subject made incarnate.' We may recall here Heidegger's famous philosophical meditation, *The Thing*, where he considers the jug as a counterpart of the void, its character determined by a core of emptiness.

For the jug Heidegger traces an ontological pathway from the origins of clay in the earth, mapping in addition a conceptual and etymological pathway of the word *thing*, revealing that the old German word *dinc* conveyed an unexpectedly rich range of meanings. *Dinc* signified a gathering; a coming together for deliberation or discourse; an 'affair or matter of pertinence.' Thus, for Heidegger, a 'thing' implies not only the object's resilient, assertive autonomy, but also its social, intersubjective context.[24] For Newman too, a found object, removed from its original purpose can become a overdetermined *Thing*. The object is transfigured into a repurposed entity: the gate now operates as a gate for our gazing, a gate for reflection, a gate for poetry.

…

More than is the case with any other artist in the current exhibition, the found object retains its autonomy in Trish Roan's artwork. A pictorial/architectural/compositional context is never presupposed in her choice of objects. Rather, the operative challenge is to devise ways of making objects belong, motivating them to enter into contexts and associations with their neighbours, and integrating them with their environs. Choosing, collecting and sifting the possibilities of re-presentation, the microcosm of the work of art could be interpreted as an allegory of the individual in society. However, the object's assimilation is never a forgone conclusion.

Indeed, Roan's art maintains a position of acute uncertainty. Because the objects' autonomy is assumed from the outset, the possibility of their interaction is necessarily limited: 'I've been accumulating some collections that may or may not become something solid – it's too early to say. I'd like them to become something, but I really don't know yet,' she says.[25]

In reviewing Bergson's ideas of creation, Bertrand Russell noted 'that evolution is truly creative, like the work of an artist. An impulse to action, an undefined want, exists beforehand, but until the want is satisfied it is impossible to know the nature of what will satisfy it.'[26] The transient qualities that Roan and her objects seek to harness are not easily *represented*. Her motivation is to bring the discarded, 'poor', unexamined aspects of the world into view and 'within reach.'[27]

'When something is so close to the everyday,' Roan says, 'I feel it has a more profound revelation. A lot of what I think about and travel towards… is about drawing something from (perceived) nothing, holding it briefly and releasing it back to 'nothing' – back into the world of things or weather or other kinds of indifference.'[28]

The function of the object is so tenuous as regards its repurposing as a work of art, that the conventional distinction imposed between presentation and representation is easily blurred or subverted. When a found object is photographed or filmed it is obviously given over to representation, whereas, when it is re-presented in a crude state, all the devices responsible for isolating, framing and intensifying focus on the object – endowing it with the aura of art – are much more elusive and open to question.

Roan's video work, *Iris* (illus. p. 28 & 29), consists of a series of photographic stills linked by the recurrent motif of a discarded elastic band. These unexceptional objects, which are never identical, suggest cells or amoebae, and through their repetition they grow ever more relational. Like the ancient Greek *omphalos*, each elastic band becomes a centre, a navel of the world. In a universe that recognises no centre, the paradox is that everything and everywhere can assert itself as a provisional centre. The elastic band is also an archetypal drawing: a circumscription. The line has its inside and outside. The imposition of a 'figure' cut out from a 'field' momentarily interrupts the 'indifference' of the pavement or footpath. Encountered in the open, abandoned, the object is exposed – porous,[29] revealing a 'conditional sense of meaning that can be disbanded at any moment' – at *every* moment.

The ripped edges and wrenched planes that constitute Erwin Fabian's sculptures seem to have the lightness and plasticity of clay. Their weight and mass are dissimulated by the volume of air invited into the heart of the assemblage. Harking back to the flashpoint of 1910 and the revelatory moment of Cubist collage, Fabian's formal language incidentally testifies to the impact that Picasso's constructions have had on precursor sculptors in the 20th Century like Julio González, Richard Stankiewicz and David Smith, and so Margit Rowell's characterisation of Cubist sculpture pertains to Fabian's work as well: 'The volumes of objects [are] translated into spatial voids. Space, once the outer envelope of sculpture, becomes its very substance.'[30] The alternation of planar elements with the intervening spaces – with the void – posits the interaction of positive and negative, inner and outer, tactile and optical inferences.

The generational link between Erwin Fabian (b. 1915) and Robert Motherwell (b. 1915), both of whom retain idiomatic connections to Abstract Expressionism and profess a deep identification with the legacy of Cubism, may also encourage us to consider similarities in their ideas. The rapport between solid and void in such works as *Bloom* (illus. p. 45) suggests a metaphysical rationalisation. We might link *Bloom's* floral/female form to a general idea of fecundity and to intimations of the 'first beginnings of things' (*primordia rerum*) or the 'seeds of things,' i.e. to Lucretian concepts so old that they have become brand new.

The torn and fractured vernacular of Fabian's constructions evoke the Lucretian dichotomy of rupture and creation – in Lucretius' own words:

'And so the destructive motions cannot hold sway eternally and bury existence forever; nor again can the motions that cause life and growth preserve created things eternally. Thus, in this war that has been waged from time everlasting, the contest between the elements is an equal one: now here, now there, the vital forces conquer and in turn, are conquered.'[31]

For Nicole Ellis, 'the idea of construction/destruction was helpful early on. It was instructive in the importance of risk-taking and being prepared to lose something in the process of finding something.' She adds: 'I am now interested in the idea of a dismantling/reorganising process, rather than the putting-back-together principle of traditional archaeology. I dismantle objects to discover how they are made, to reveal their hidden structure.'[32]

From an early phase in her history, Ellis realised that primary invention, making something out of nothing, went against her creative predilections. The found object and, more specifically, found materials have provided the initial stimulus for more diverse avenues of invention. In her recent *Time-Lapse* series (illus. p. 40 & 41) she alters the character of already coloured, already textured fabrics, extracting from them the most unexpected evocations of space, light and air. The constituent fabrics are laminated and torn apart, displaying the residues of the adhesives which streak and mottle their blues and greys with bright cloud formations. Subtle, almost subliminal tints modify the coloured ground: they are the residues left by ripping apart differently coloured textiles. As with Peter Atkins, Ellis' role is virtually that of an editor, a compiler, a tailor of elegant formal constructs.

Ellis' seemingly vaporous distillations emit an energy of transformation. The suspended integers elicit a microphysical propensity, bring to mind the atomic thresholds of visibility whilst equally extending to encompass the immensity of space.

Colour is central to Ellis' art. Found colour in the form of used, flawed or modified fabrics provides her with a ready-made palette. Ellis' configurations of colour elide into voluminous illusions of light. This leads us to recall Lucretius' account of vision in which air 'passes through our eyes,' or 'luminous air… filled up the pathways of the eye with light.'[33] It is through light, the enabler of colour and the conduit of an endless stream of atoms, that we are able to envisage the contents of the void.

For Robert Motherwell, each blank canvas or sheet of paper presented a void, and this primordial emptiness precipitated the birth of a new creation. Recalling the phrase of Mallarmé's, 'the whiteness of the paper defends,' Motherwell confessed to his difficulty in beginning work and his anxiety that a work might not live up to the perfect unity it displaces and supersedes.[34] One approach, also prescribed by Mallarmé, was the method of chance, a 'throw of the dice' whereby an arbitrary intervention provokes a chain of catalytic reactions. As with the three lithographs, *Harvest with orange stripe* (illus. p. 33), *Harvest with blue shadow* and *Pauillac no. 4,* the found object sets a tonic note within the composition and a call and response ensues. The artist's efforts to accommodate the foreign fragment endow it with strategic, relational value, so that the observer, in a Bergsonian sense, becomes 'capable of reflecting upon the object and of enlarging it indefinitely.'[35]

As a young man Motherwell studied philosophy at Stanford and Harvard. Historians and scholars have tended to overlook the relevance of his academic grounding until recently. Motherwell's interest in art lay in the primary process of creation and he attributed this to one of the fundamental insights of the Cubists. He wrote:

'Working with great intelligence, stubbornness and objectivity, they stumbled over the leading insight of the 20th century: all thought and feeling is relative to man, he does not reflect the world but invents it.'[36]

Cubist imaging fed into Motherwell's reading of Bergson's vitalism, John Dewey's sense of immediacy and – most of all – the metaphysics of Alfred North Whitehead.[37] In *Process and Reality*, Whitehead outlined a scheme in which process, or what we might prefer to call events, are the fundamental make-up of reality. He proposed a perpetual state of 'becoming' in which actual entities or occasions result from the *concrescence* of all elements within the scheme. He wrote: 'It lies in the nature of things that the many enter into complex unity.'[38] Motherwell understood 'that "meaning" was a product of relations among elements'[39] that can be apprehended in collage's 'capacity to arrive':

'No wonder the artist is constantly placing and displacing, relating and rupturing relations: his task is to find a complex of qualities whose feeling is just right – veering towards the unknown and chaos, yet ordered and related in order to be apprehended.'[40]

Motherwell's *America – La France* series (see illus. 39 & 44) re-fathoms the processes of a universal scheme defined by dialectical fields of tension. Transcending multiplicity, 'the many become one, and are increased by one'[41] as the new entity *becomes*. From the initial disorder the artist intuits a 'relational structure,' and his instinct directs the work *'toward the realisation of a potential order*.'[42] Formerly dispersed elements achieve a newfound bonding. In Whitehead's terms, this forms a 'unified actuality … devoid of all indetermination.

Potentiality has passed into realisation. They are complete and determinate matter of fact, devoid of all indecision.'[43]

Like the early collages of Picasso and Braque, some of these works were initially conceived as a model – as preliminary steps towards a final print edition – yet each work has its own vitality and bears the imprint of a brilliant creative mind. Viewed as a developing concept, *America – La France* speaks of its own temporality and passage: the movement from one state to another tends to emphasise the provisional nature of each successive image and suggests a formative process that, in other realms of life, establishes identity and determines existence.

Donald Kuspit, responding to the insights of Alfred North Whitehead, identified collage as a metaphor for the 'principle of universal relativity.'[44] He wrote: 'Collage, for the first time in art, makes uncertainty a method of creation, apparent indeterminacy a procedure… its unity as much in the potentiality of its becoming as in the actuality of its presence.'[45] For Matt Arbuckle, found sheets of paper motivate his compositional adventures, providing a surprising stimulus or an unfamiliar foundation. 'When working over found paper' he says, 'I am always responding to what already exists.'[46]

As with Trish Roan, Arbuckle's found materials are often chosen for their immediacy, their poignant marginality and valuelessness: they are social outcasts devoid of preciousness, their markings perhaps fresher and more exhilarating than could be achieved by any hand of intent.

Densely blue technical drawings provide the ground for *In Between* and *Sliding Door Opportunity* (illus. p. 46-47 & 12-13). A counterpart is set up by Arbuckle's arrangement of slashing integers or rectangular sheets of white and off-white paper marked with daubed accumulations of non-colour. The opposition of these anonymous, artless smudges with the obviously skilled and unalterable figuration of the blueprints raises questions about aesthetic sufficiency and the relationship of images to the hand, the body and the eye.

The blueprint is perfect but dead – whereas the crude markings have the potential to evolve and associate. However, the viewer may not be able to decide whether the collaged elements evidence a meaningless scrawl or the artist's deliberate marks, whether these markings are accidental or intentional. Nonetheless they contribute vigour, warmth and accessibility to the collages, bringing them within the viewer's reach.

The dialectic of the parts qualifies the arrival of the whole. As Kuspit notes, 'The elements are already "relative" by reason of their displacement from the life-world into the "art world" and by reason of their fragmentary state. Taken together, seen relative to one another, their relativity seems irresistible and fundamental.'[47]

Here, the poet Charles Olson's discussion of poetic composition through projective, open verse provides a useful parallel:

'From the moment he ventures into field composition – puts himself in the open – he can go by no track other than the one the poem under hand declares … it is a matter, finally of OBJECTS, what they are, what they are inside a poem, how they got there, and once there, how they are to be used… Every element… must be taken up as participants in the kinetics of the poem… must be handled … in such a way that a series of tensions (which they also are) are made to *hold*, and to hold exactly inside the content and the context of the poem which has forced itself, through the poet and them, into being.'[48]

Arbuckle's works on paper, like all the art in the current exhibition, manifest 'a suspended moment' or what Braque called an 'in-between.' As Braque explained:

'You see, I have made a discovery: I no longer believe in anything. Objects don't exist for me except in so far as a rapport exists between them or between them and myself. In other words, it is not the objects that matter to me but what is in between them; it is this "in-between" that is the real subject of my pictures. When one attains this harmony, one reaches a sort of intellectual non-existence – what I can only describe as a state of perfect freedom and peace – which makes everything possible and right. Life then becomes a perpetual revelation. That is true poetry.'[49]

'For the painter, for the poet, for artists (this is what makes them different from other men, and especially from scientists), each work becomes a new universe with its own laws.' – Guillaume Apollinaire[50]

…

Anthony Oates
Curator, Exhibitions
Drill Hall Gallery
Australian National University, Canberra
October 2016

1 Braque in conversation with Dora Vallier 1954, quoted in Dan Grigorescu (trans. Richard Hillard), *Braque* (London: Murrays, 1977), p. 11.
2 Guillaume Apollinaire, *Les Peintres Cubistes: Méditations Ésthétiques* (Paris, 17 March 1913) in Mark Antliff and Patricia Leighten (eds), *A Cubist Reader: Documents and Criticism 1906-1914* (Chicago: University of Chicago Press, 2008), p. 482.
3 Francis Ponge, *Braque* (New York: H.N. Abrams, 1971), p. 57.
4 Others in this circle include André Martinet, Gustave Guillaume and Emile Benveniste. For an analysis of Saussure's analogous discoveries to the Cubists', see Yve-Alain Bois, 'Kahnweiler's Lesson', *Representations* no. 18 (1987), p. 48-52.
5 See Richard Shiff, *Doubt - Theories of Modernism and Post Modernism in the Visual Arts* (New York: Routledge, 2008).
6 'Conversation avec Picasso', *Cahiers d'art*, vol. 10, no. 10 (1935), quoted in Ellen H. Johnson, *Modern Art and the Object* (London: Thames and Hudson, 1976), p. 10.
7 George Charbonnier, *Monologue du peintre: entretiens avec Braque*, quoted in Peter Daysan, *Art as Music, Music as Poetry, Poetry as Art* (Surrey: Ashgate, 2011), p. 79.
8 Artist correspondence with the author (questionnaire, 3 June 2016).
9 Henri Bergson (trans. Nancy Margaret Paul and W. Scott Palmer), *Matter and Memory*, (New York: Macmillan Co, 1911), p. xii. https://archive.org/details/matterandmemory00berguoft (22 August 2016).
10 Bertrand Russell, 'Philosophy of Bergson', *The Monist*, vol. 22 (1912), p. 341. https://archive.org/details/jstor-27900381 (22 August 2016).
11 Rudolf Arnheim, *Entropy and art: An Essay on Disorder and Order* (Berkeley: University of California Press, 1971), p. 43.
12 James Boswell, *The Life of Samuel Johnson*, p. 387. Quoted by the artist in correspondence with the author (questionnaire, 7 August 2016).
13 Correspondence with the author, *ibid.*
14 Henri Bergson (trans. Arthur Mitchell), *Creative Evolution* (New York: Henry Holt and Company, 1911), p. 319. https://archive.org/details/creativeevolu1st00berguoft (22 August 2016).
15 *ibid.*, p. 390.
16 Henri Bergson, *Mind and Matter*, *op. cit.*, p. vii.
17 Guillaume Apollinaire, *Les Peintres Cubistes: Méditations Ésthétiques, op. cit.*, p. 478.
18 Guillaume Apollinaire, 'Georges Braque', *Exposition Georges Braque* (9-28 November 1908, Galerie Kahnweiler, Paris), quoted in Mark Antliff and Patricia Leighten (eds), *op. cit.*, p. 43.
19 See translation in Peter Daysan, *op. cit.*, p. 24.
20 Works such as Braque's *The Portuguese Guitar Player* (1911) are clear in their structural reference to portrayals of the Virgin and Child – an immaculate conception.
21 Correspondence with the author 7 June 2016, following quotes are from this source unless noted.
22 Francis Ponge, *op. cit.*, p. 68.
23 This idea was proposed by Guillaume Apollinaire in *Les Peintres Cubistes: Méditations Ésthétiques, op. cit.*, p. 482.
24 See Martin Heidegger (trans. Albert Hofstader), 'The Thing', *Poetry, Language, Thought* (1971), pp. 163-184. http://people.ischool.berkeley.edu/~ryanshaw/nmwg/the.thing-heidegger.pdf (3 July 2016).
25 Correspondence with the author 5 June 2016, following quotes are from this source unless noted.
26 Bertrand Russell, *op. cit.*, p. 323.
27 Georges Braque, quoted in John Richardson, *Georges Braque* (London: Oldbourne, 1961), p. 10.
28 Artist correspondence with the author (questionnaire, 5 August 2016).
29 We may recall the poet Paul Valéry's *Le Cimetière marin* (1920), in which he wrote: 'My presence is porous.'
30 Margit Rowell, *The Planar Dimension: Europe 1912-13* (New York: Solomon Guggenheim Foundation, 1979), p. 9.
31 Lucretius, *De rerum natura* (2.569-80) quoted in Stephen Greenblatt, *The Swerve* (New York: WW Norton & Company, 2011), p. 186.
32 Artist correspondence with the author (questionnaire, 15 August 2016).
33 Quote in McGrath, Hugh P., and Comenetz, Michael, *Currents in Comparative Romance Languages and Literatures : Valéry's Graveyard: Le Cimetière marin Translated, Described, and Peopled* (New York: Peter Lang Publishing Inc., 2013) ProQuest ebrary. Web. 1 July 2016, p. 138.
34 Interview with David Sylvester 1960, quoted in Mary Ann Caws, *Robert Motherwell* (Reaktion Books, 2013), p. 100.
35 Henri Bergson, *Creative Evolution*, *op. cit.*, p. 186.
36 Robert Motherwell, 'Preliminary notice', Daniel-Henry Kahnweiler, *The Rise of Cubism* (New York: Wittenborn, Schultz Inc, 1949), p. vii.
37 See Manfred Milz, 'Essay in honor of Robert Motherwell's centenary', *Journal of Aesthetics & Culture*, vol. 8 (2016), http://dx.doi.org/10.3402/jac.v8.29952 (15 July 2016).
38 Alfred North Whitehead, *Process and Reality* (New York: Macmillan, 1929), p. 31.
39 Robert Motherwell, 'Interview with Bryan Robertson, Addenda' (1965), in Stephanie Terenzio (ed), *The Collected Writings of Robert Motherwell* (Los Angeles: University of California Press, 1999), p. 142.
40 Robert Motherwell, 'Beyond the Aesthetic' (1946), in Dore Ashton and Joan Banach (eds), *The Writings of Robert Motherwell* (Los Angeles: University of California Press, 2007), p. 54.
41 Alfred North Whitehead, *op. cit.*, p. 32.
42 Rudolf Arnheim, *op. cit.*, p. 22.
43 Alfred North Whitehead, *op. cit.*, p. 44.
44 *ibid.*, p. 33.
45 Donald B. Kuspit, 'Collage: the organising principle of art in the age of the relativity of art', in Diane Waldman (ed.), *Mestres del collage : de Picasso a Rauschenberg* (Barcelona : Fundació Joan Miró, 2005), p. 277.
46 Artist's correspondence with the author (questionnaire, 1 August 2016), following quotes from this source unless nooted.
47 Donald B Kuspit, *op. cit.*, p. 277.
48 Charles Olson, *Projective Verse* (1950), http://writing.upenn.edu/~taransky/Projective_Verse.pdf (12 August 2016).
49 in John Richardson, *op. cit.*, p. 24.
50 Guillaume Apollinaire, 'Georges Braque,' *op. cit.*, p. 45.

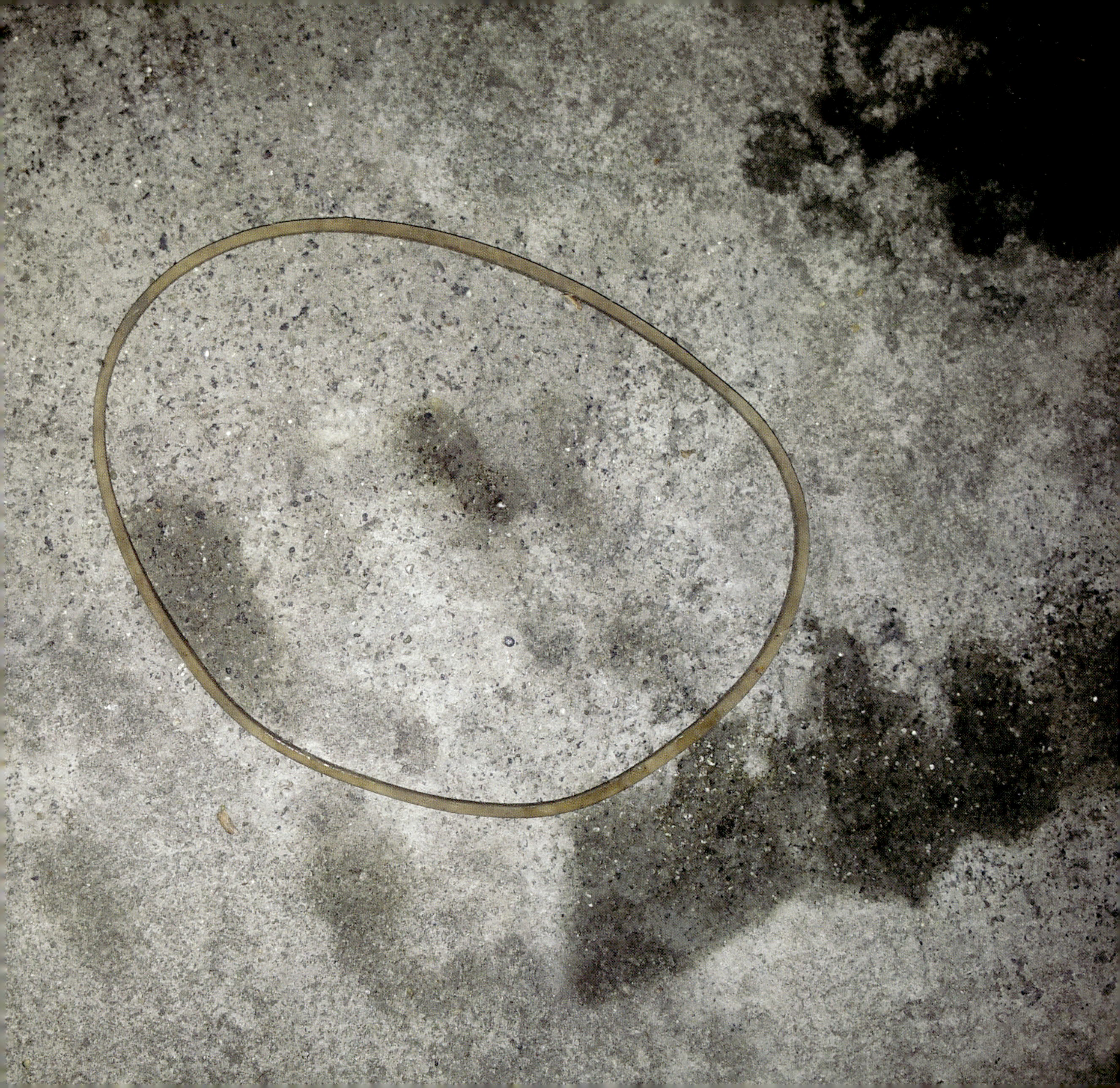

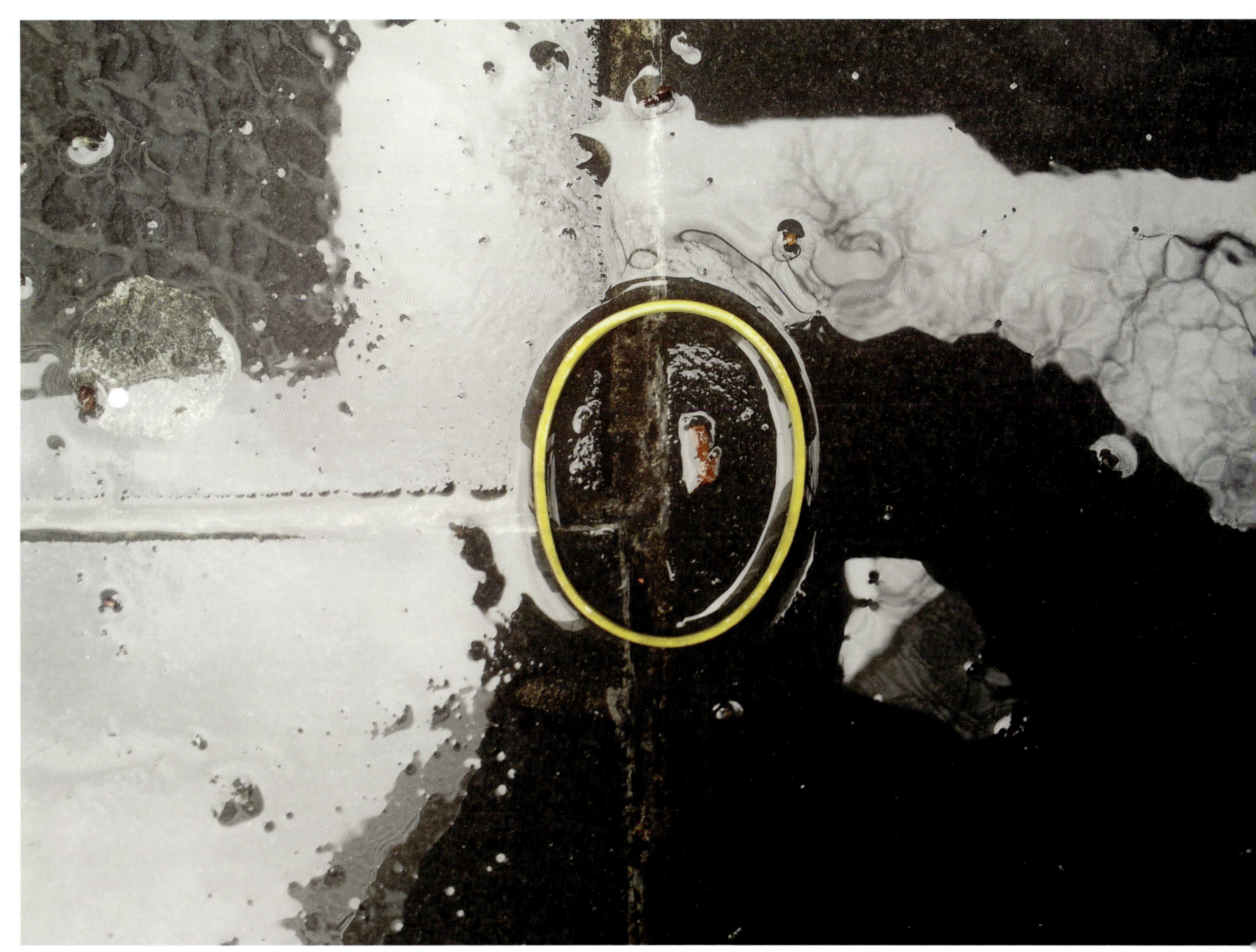

Trish Roan, *Iris*, 2016 stills (cat no 54)

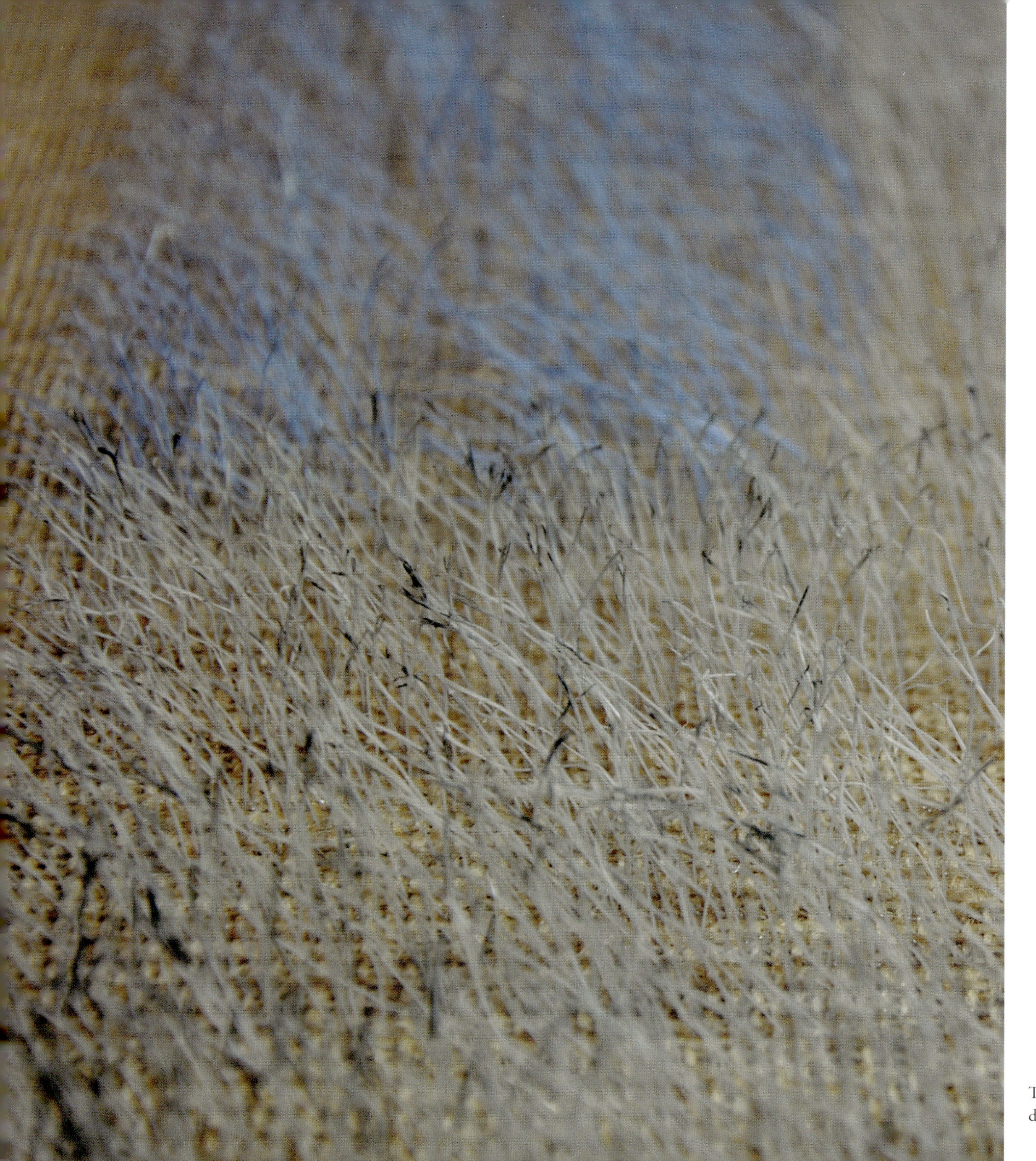

Trish Roan, Field, 2016
detail (cat no 55)

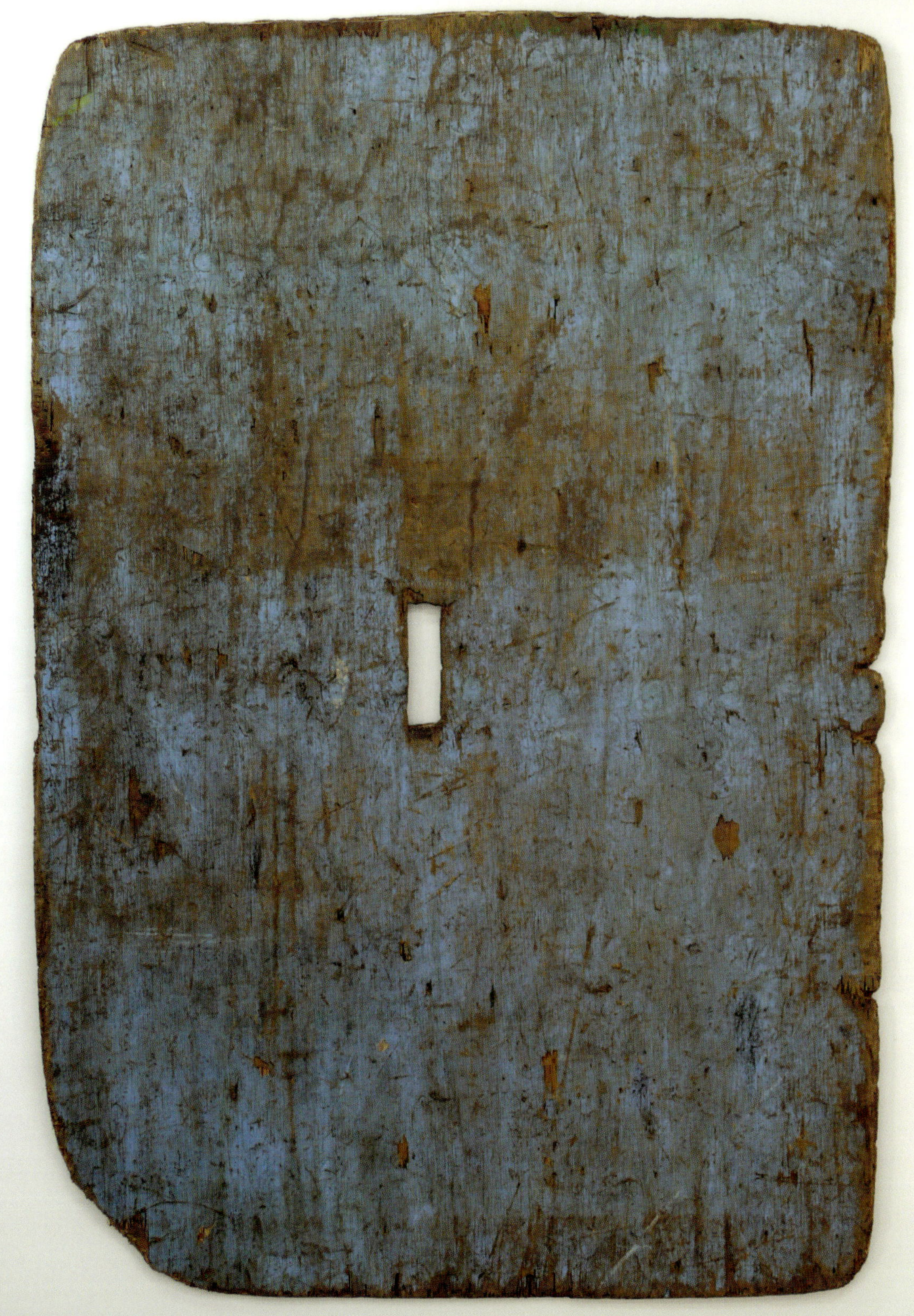

Elizabeth Newman,
Untitled, 2008 (cat no 45)

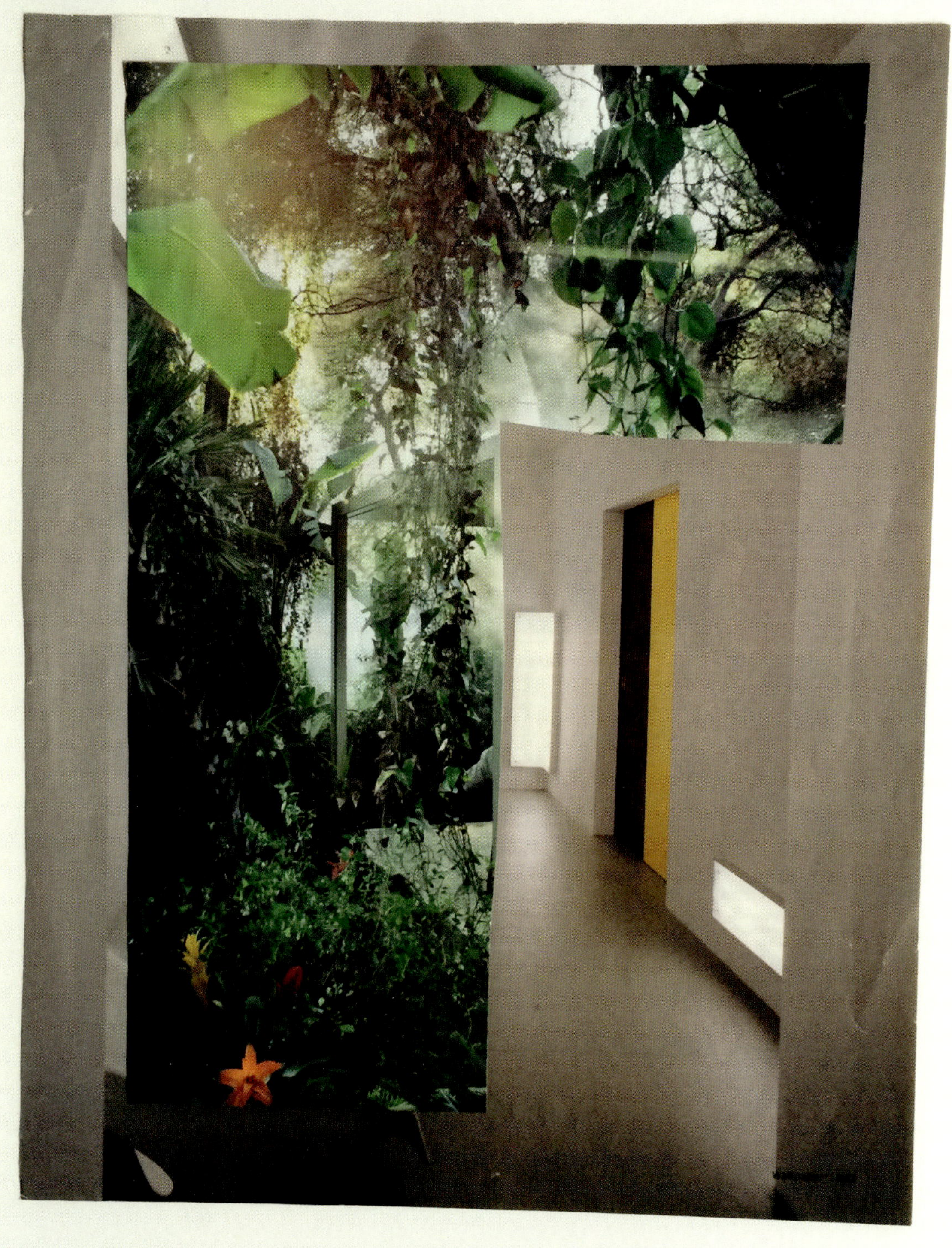

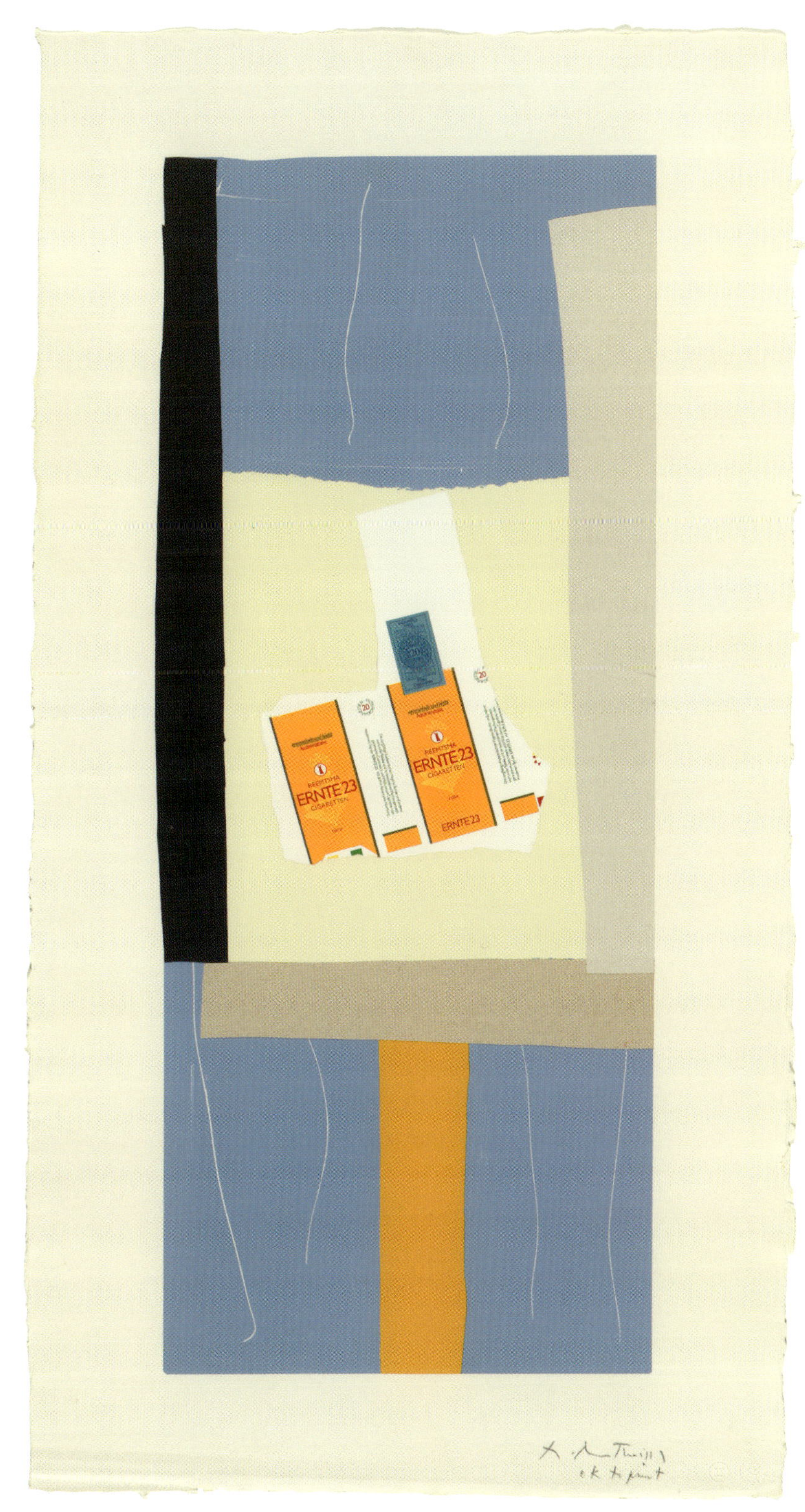

Robert Motherwell, *Harvest with orange stripe (from 'Summer light' series)*, 1973 (cat no 35); opposite: Elizabeth Newman, *Untitled*, 2014 (cat no 50)

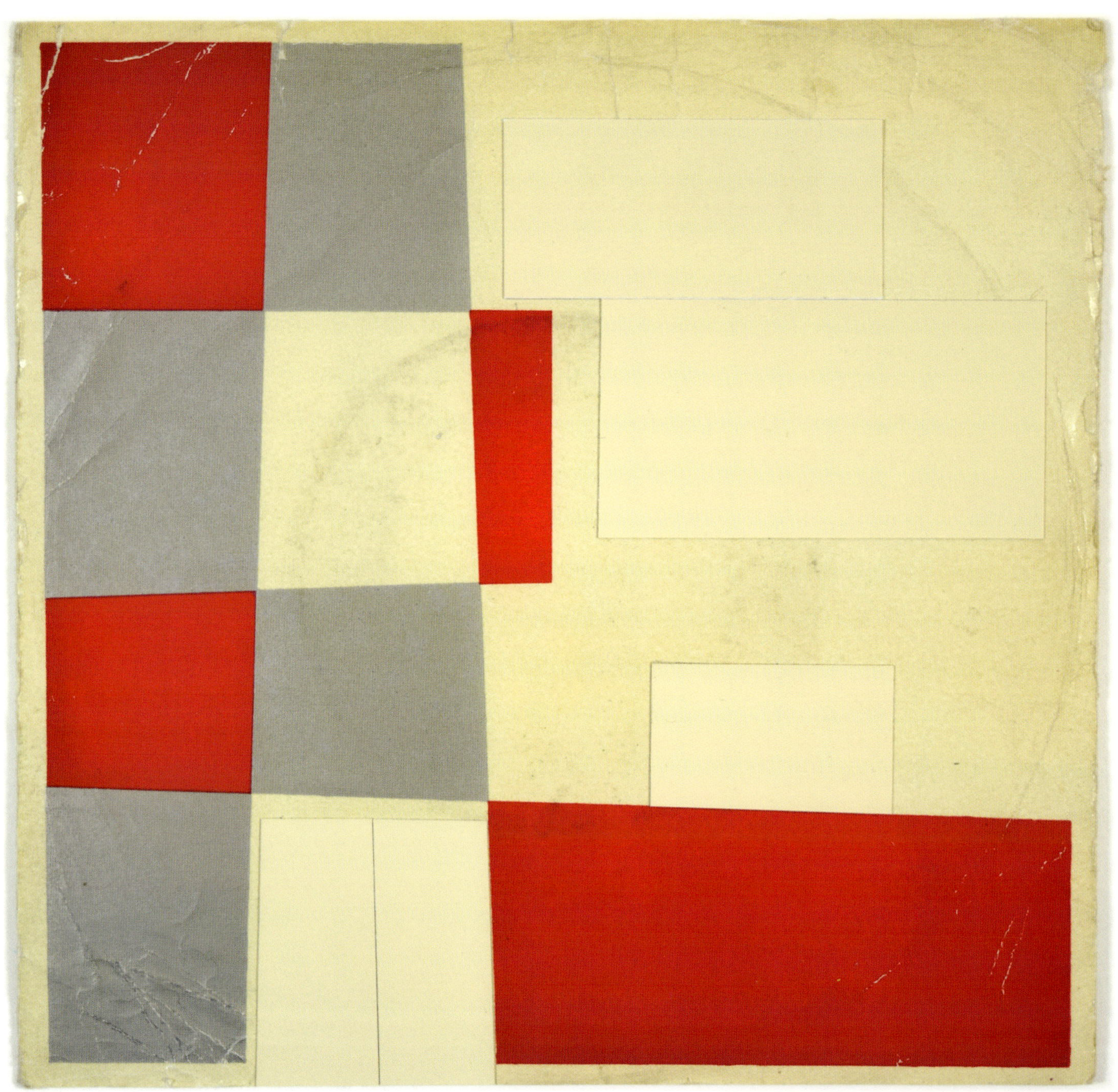

above: Peter Atkins, *Let's get Together (EP Project)*, 2015-16; opposite: *Pat Boone (EP Project)*, 2015-16 (cat no 9)

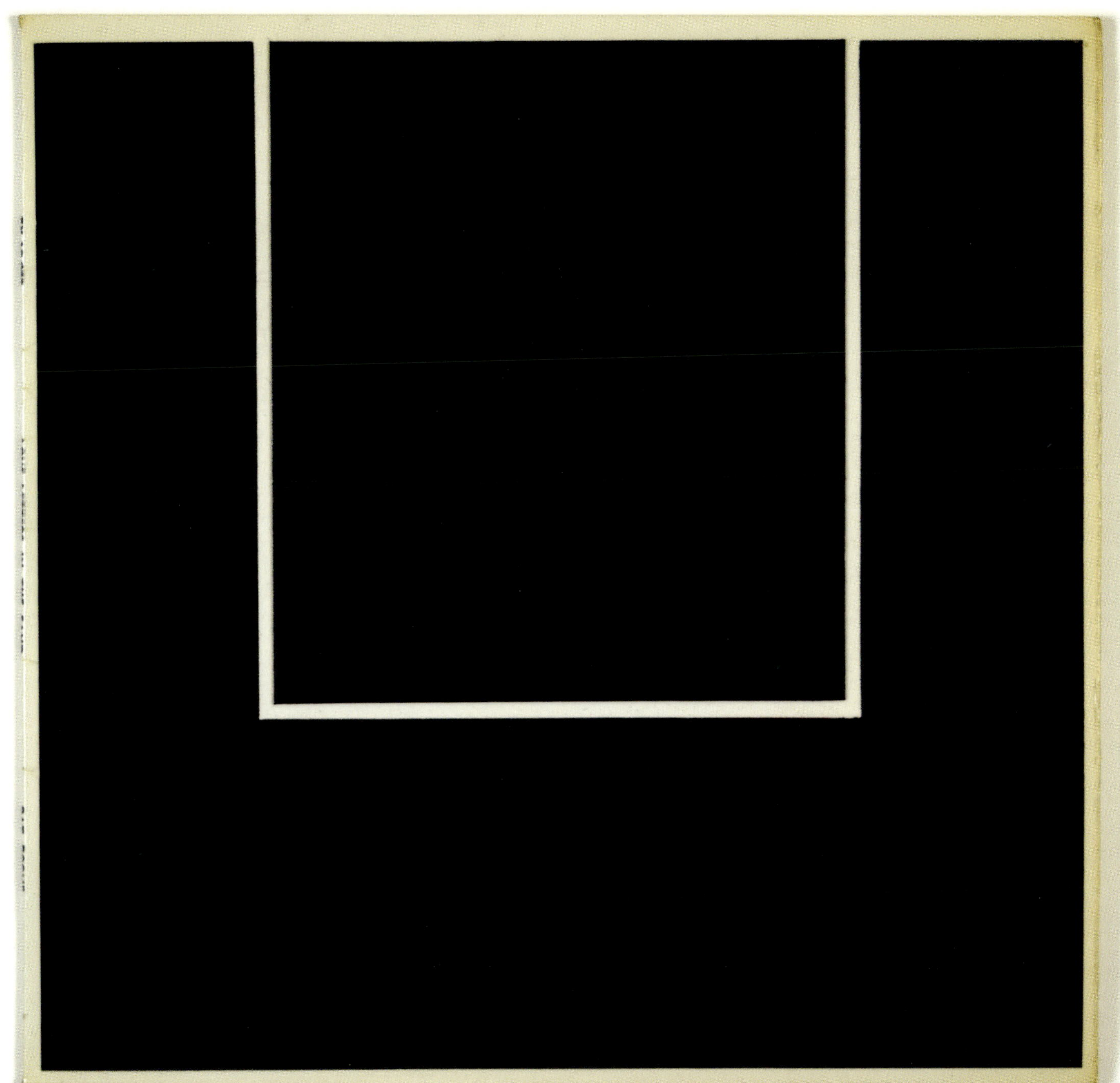

above: Chris Carmody, *Back of a Painting*, 2016 (cat no 16); opposite: *State 150 TOD*, 2016 (cat no 14)

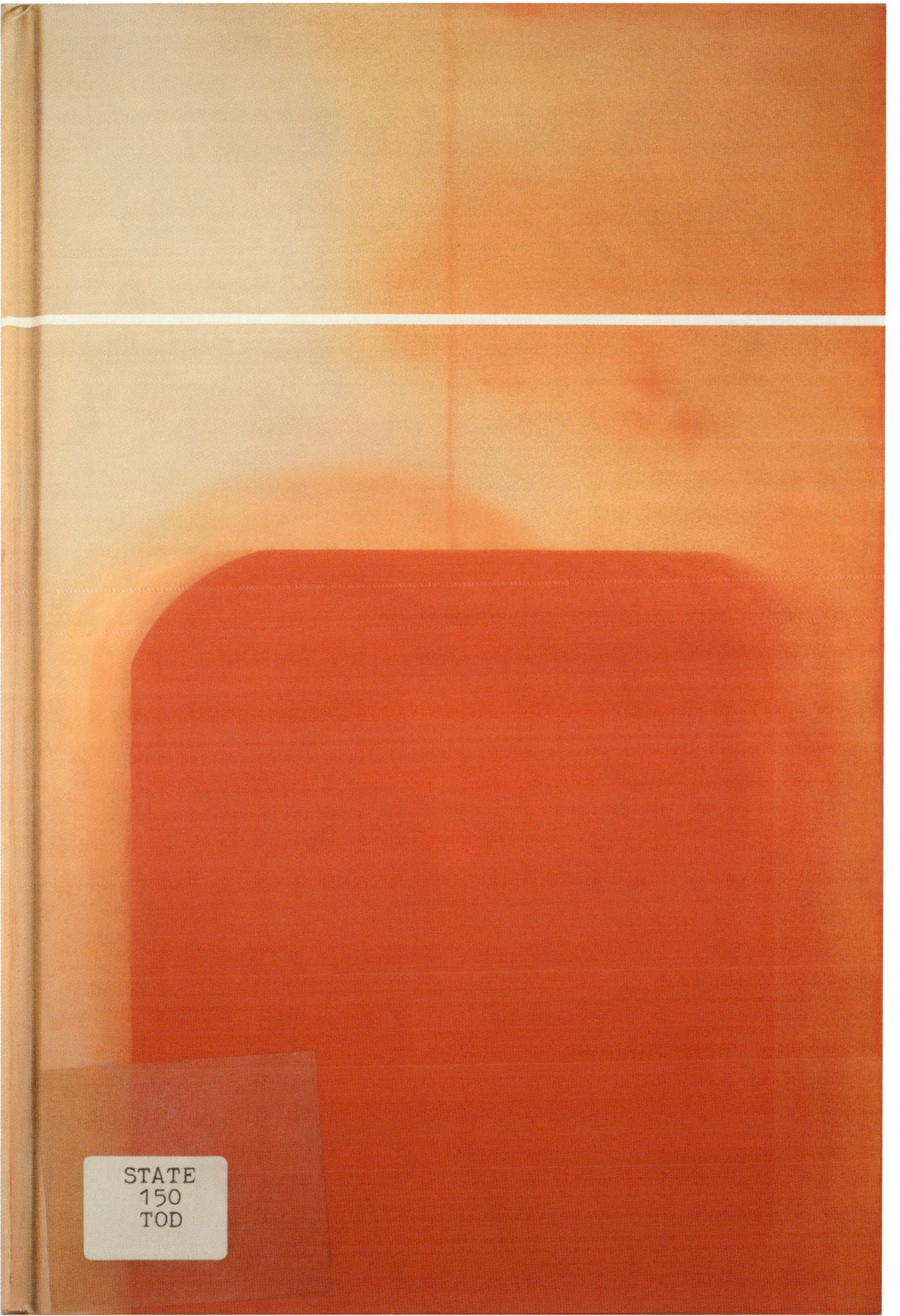
STATE
150
TOD

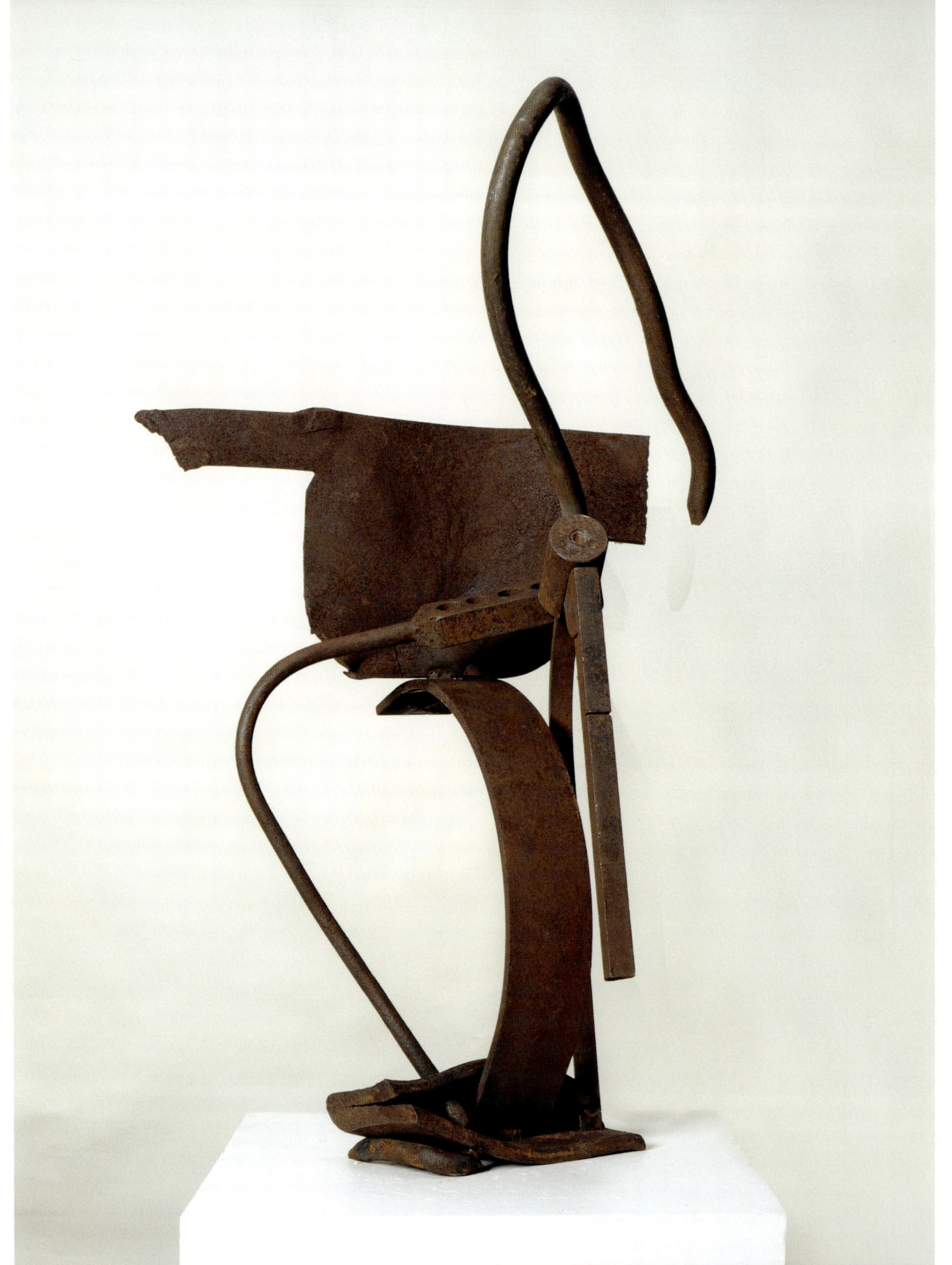

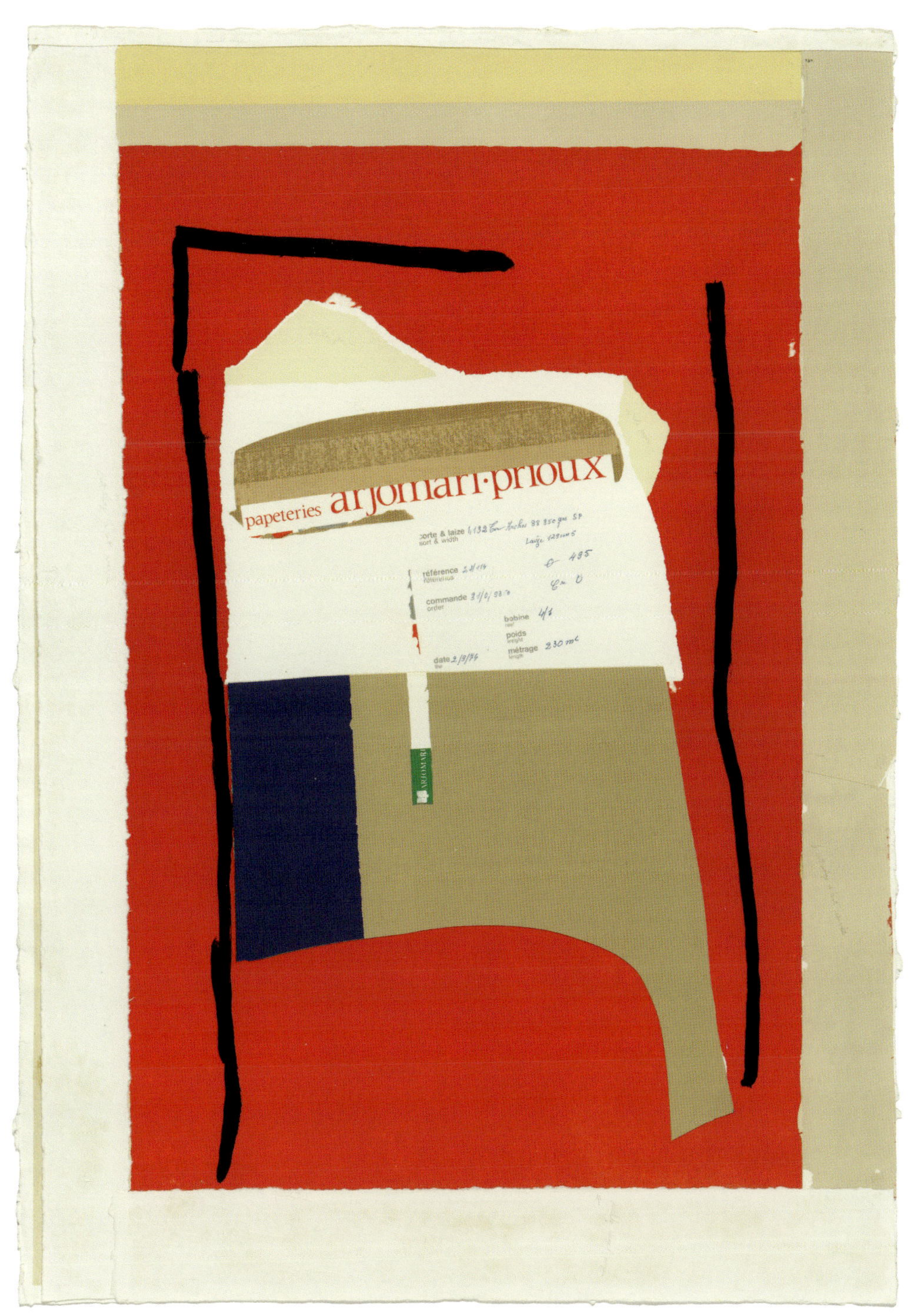

above: Robert Motherwell, *America – La France variations I,* 1983 (cat no 38); opposite: Erwin Fabian, *Epigram*, 2015 (cat no 34)

above: Nicole Ellis, *Time-Lapse 9*, 2016 (cat no 30); opposite: *Time-Lapse 8,* 2016 (cat no 29)

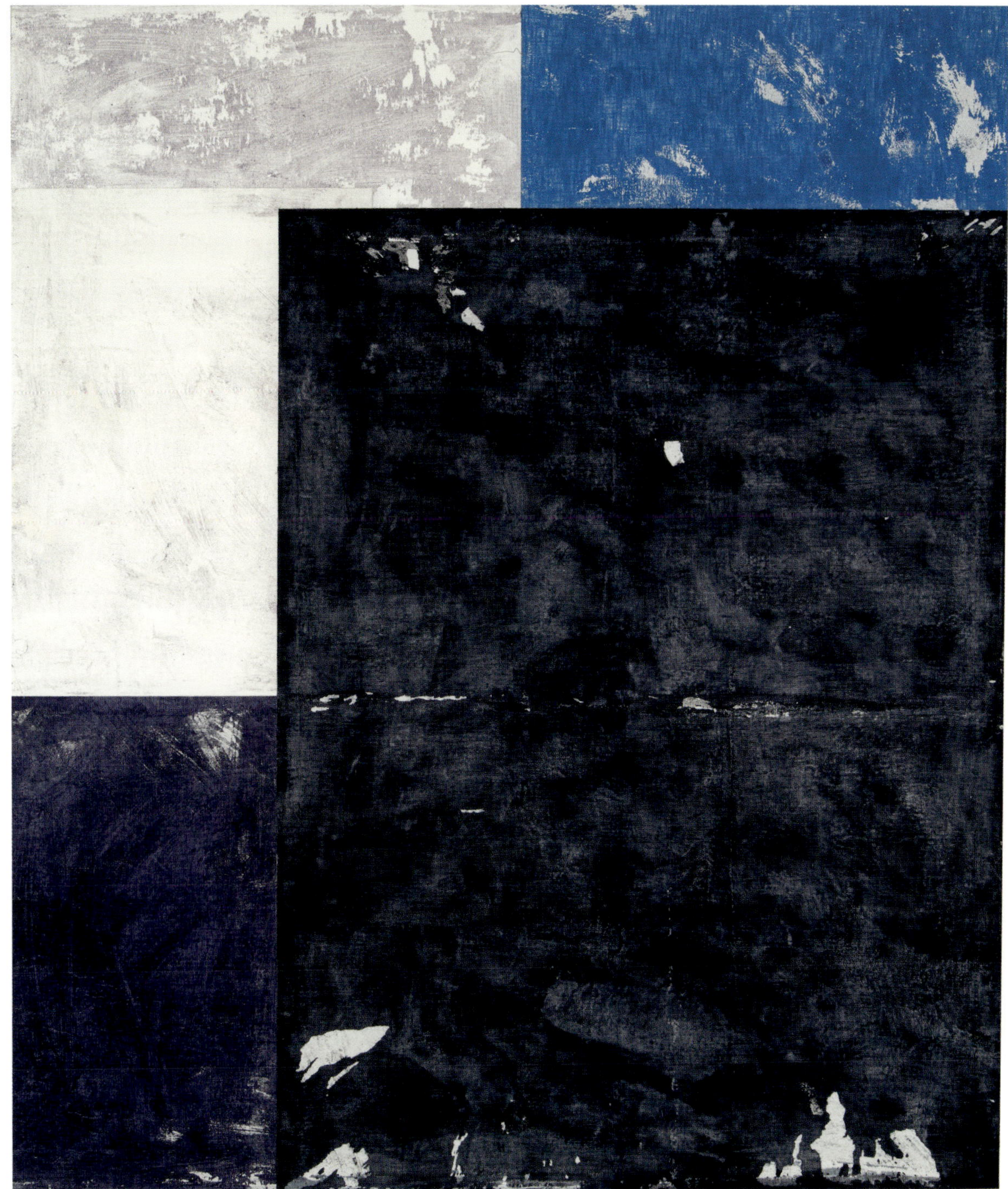

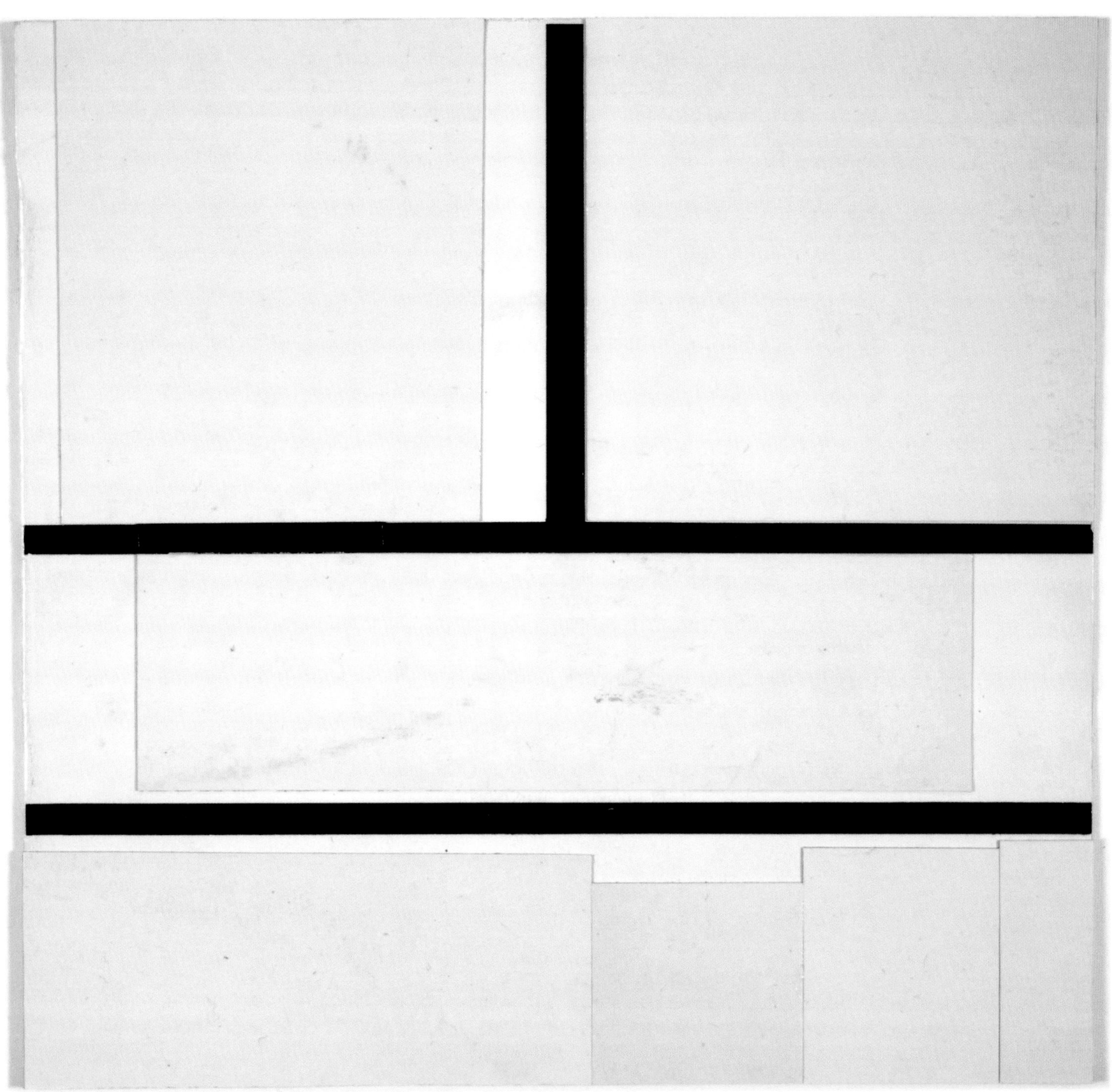

above: Peter Atkins, *Two Little Owls (EP Project)*, 2015-16 (cat no 9); opposite: Elizabeth Newman, *Jazzy One*, 2009 (cat no 47)

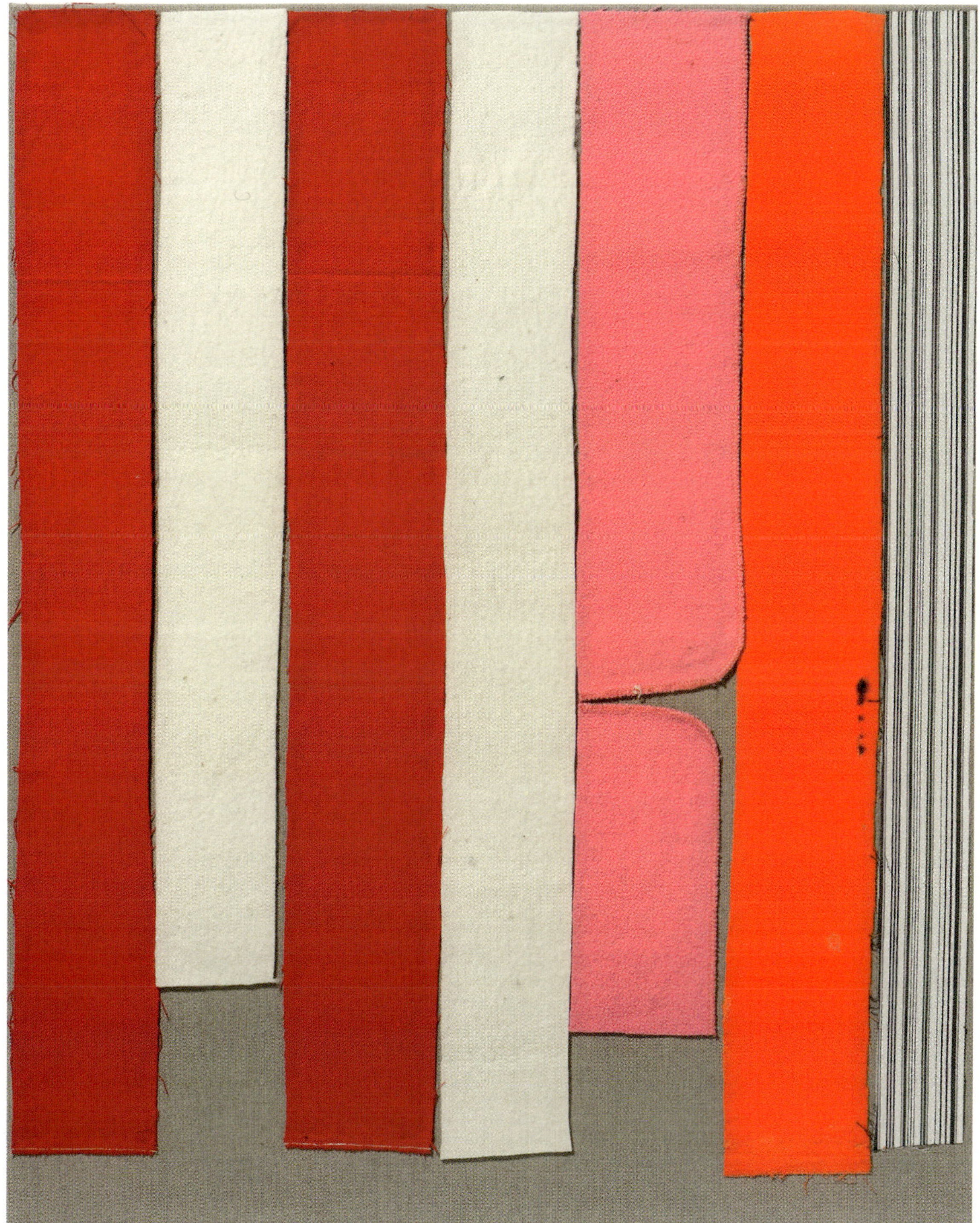

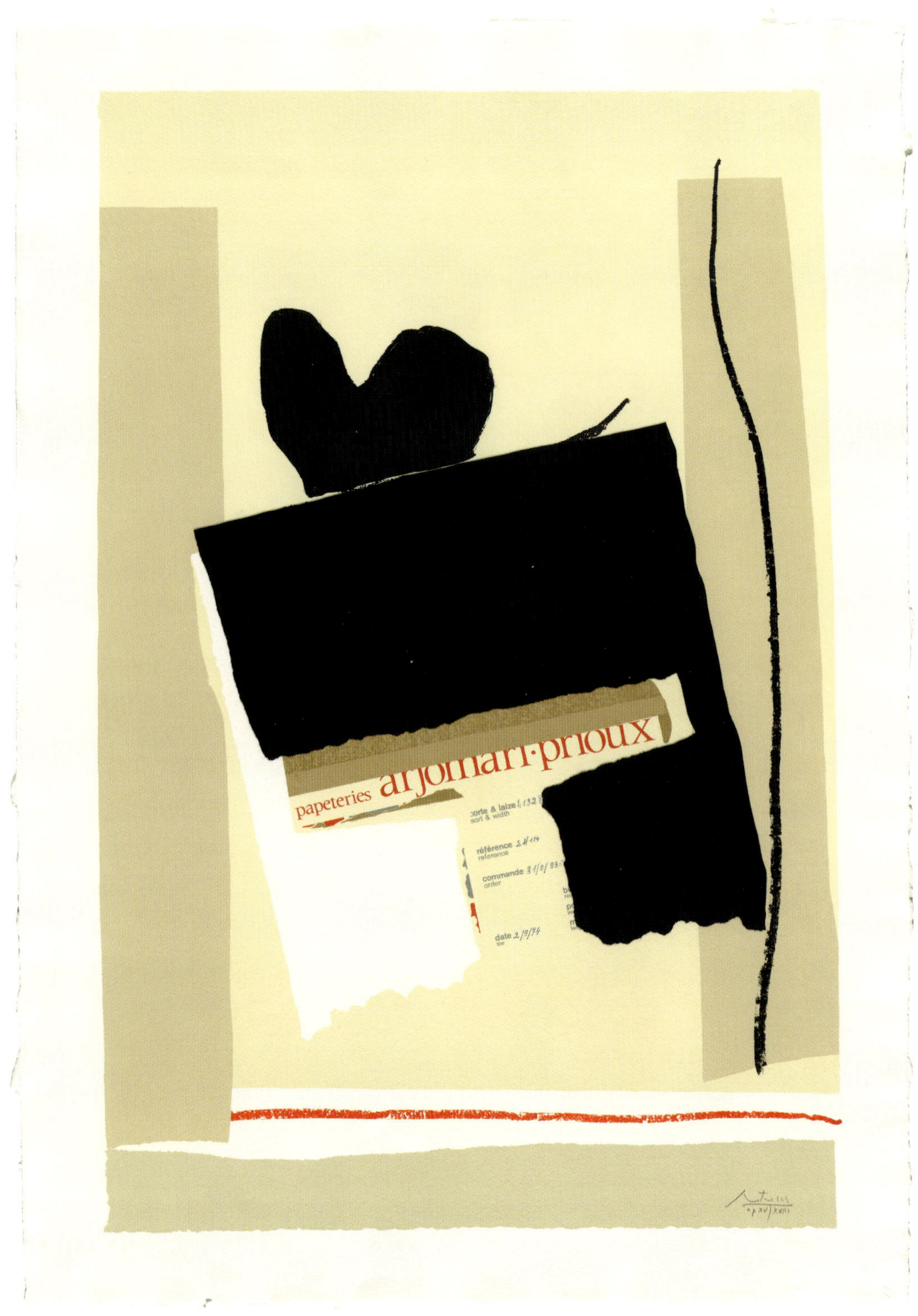

above: Robert Motherwell, *America – La France variations IV*, 1983 (cat no 39);
opposite: Erwin Fabian, *Bloom*, 2010 (cat no 33)

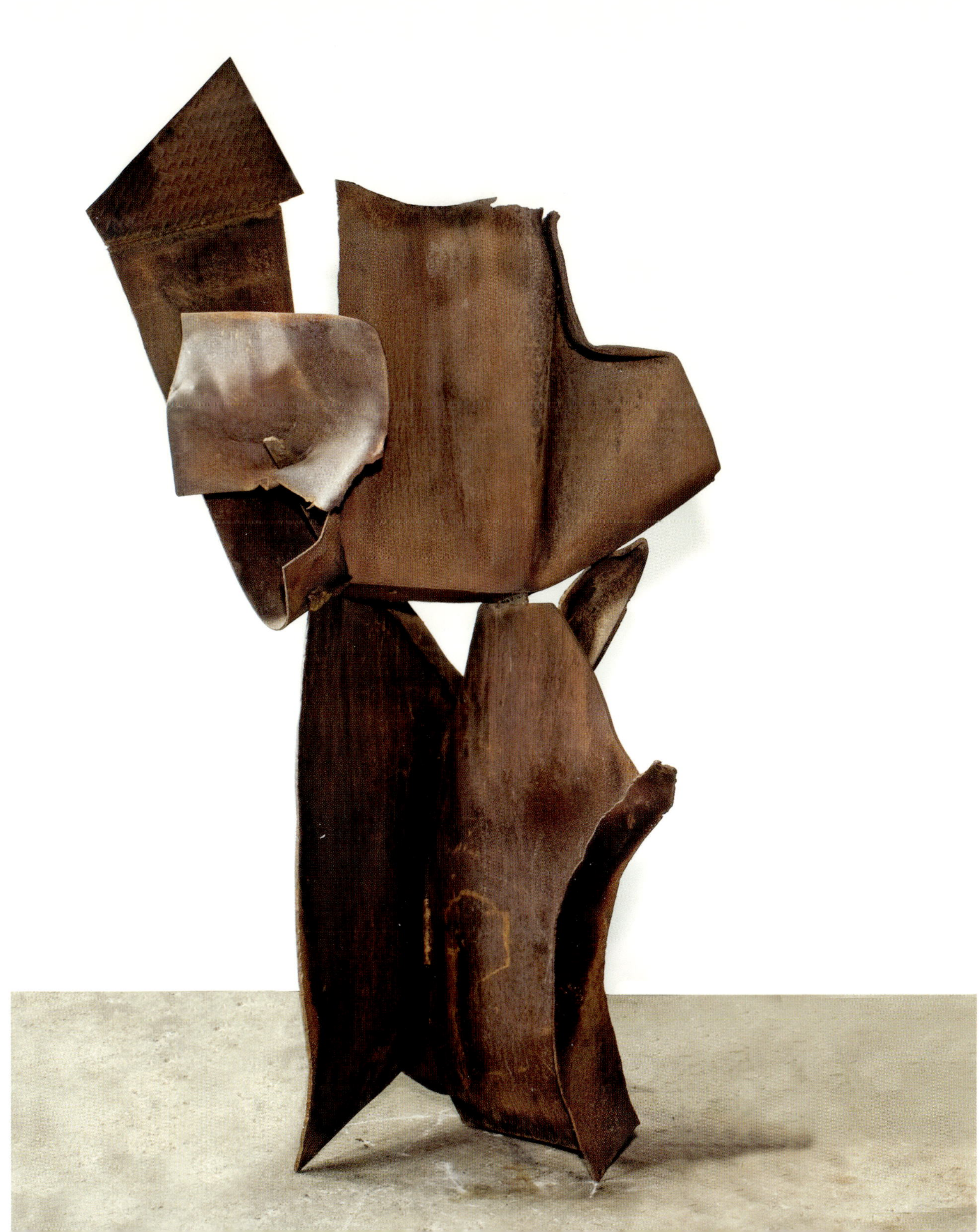

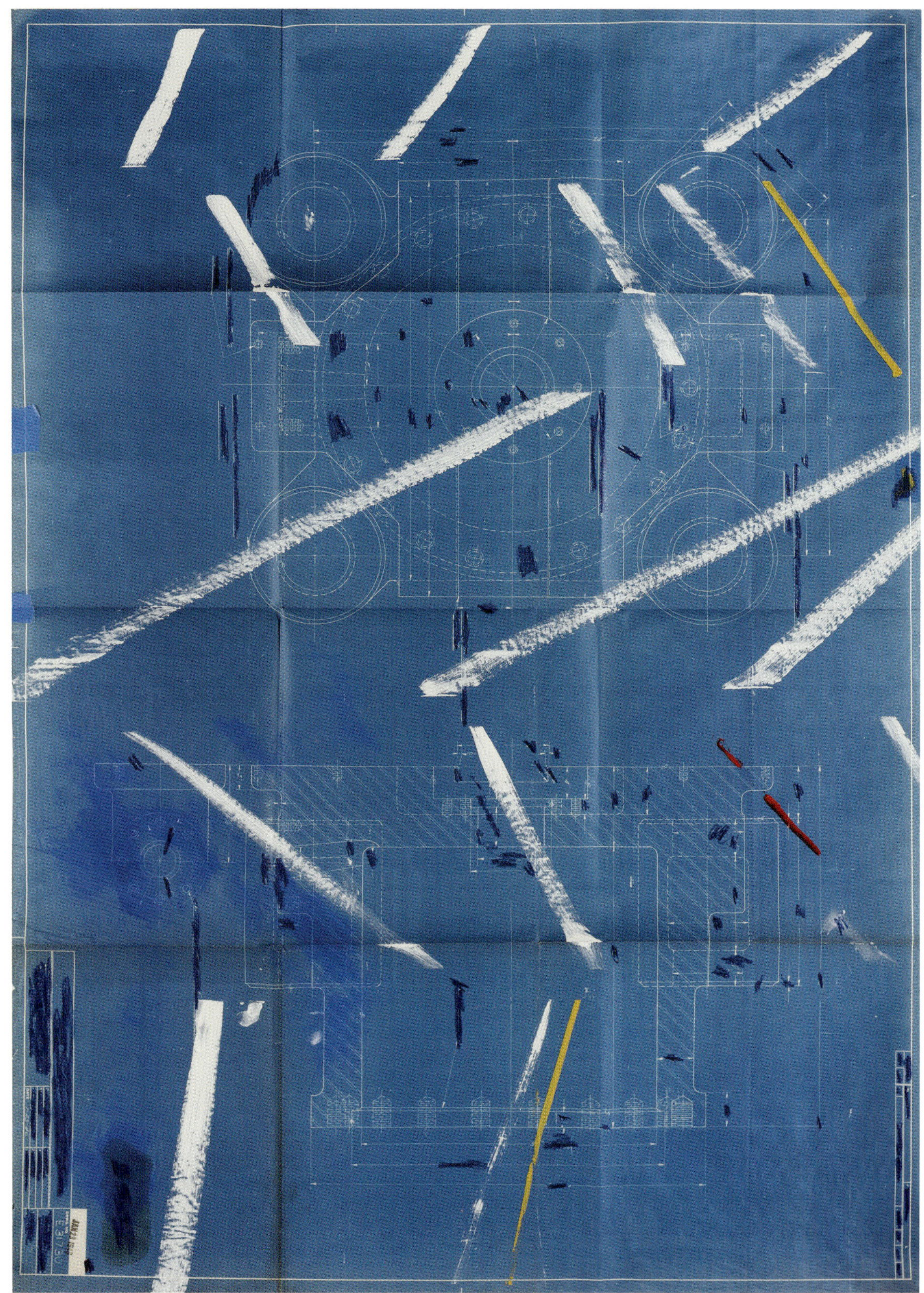

Matt Arbuckle, *In Between*, 2016 (cat no 2)

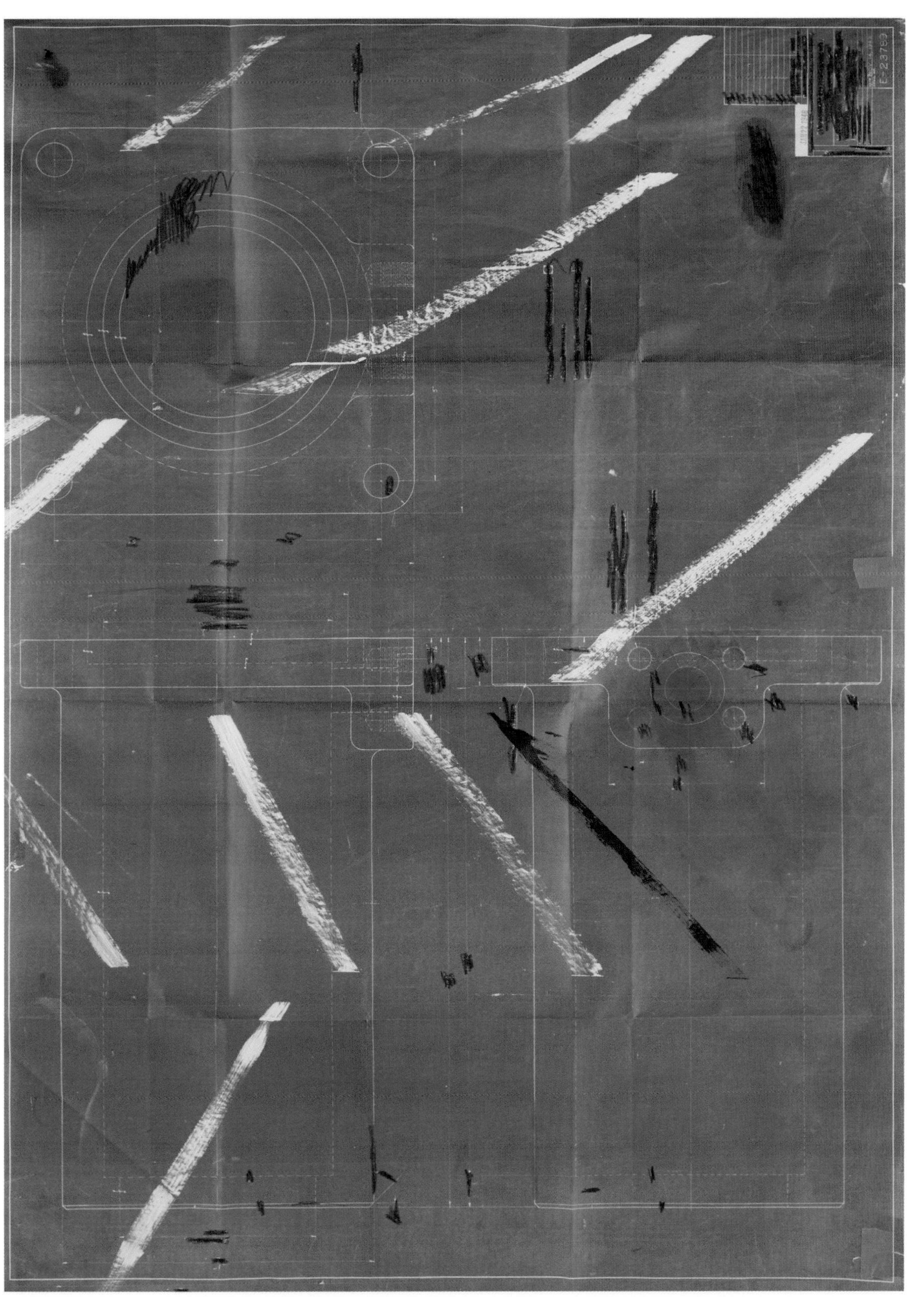

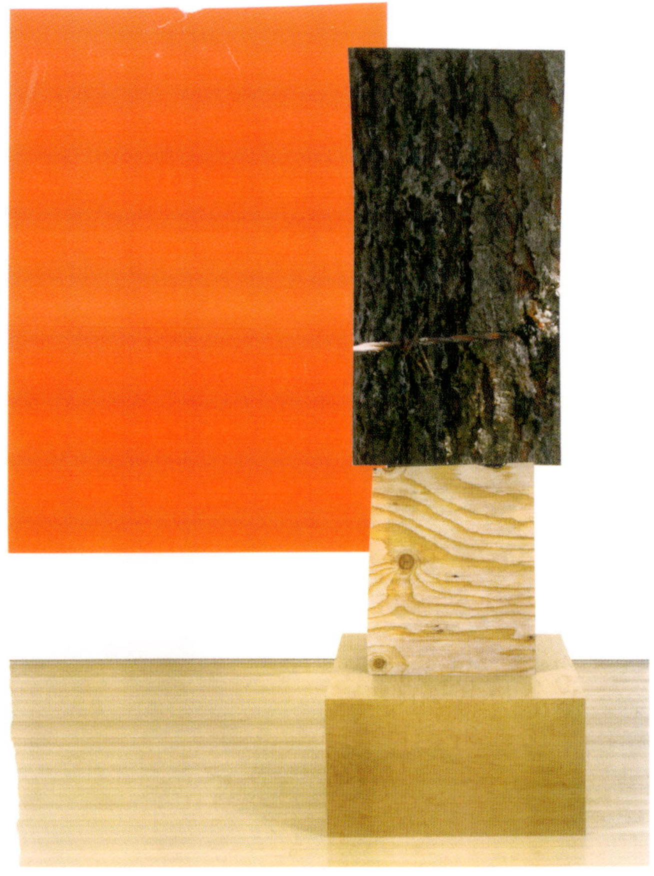

Elizabeth Newman, *Immaterial space isn't necessarily ethically superior 2*, 2012 (cat no 49); *Blanket Painting*, 2002 (cat no 43)

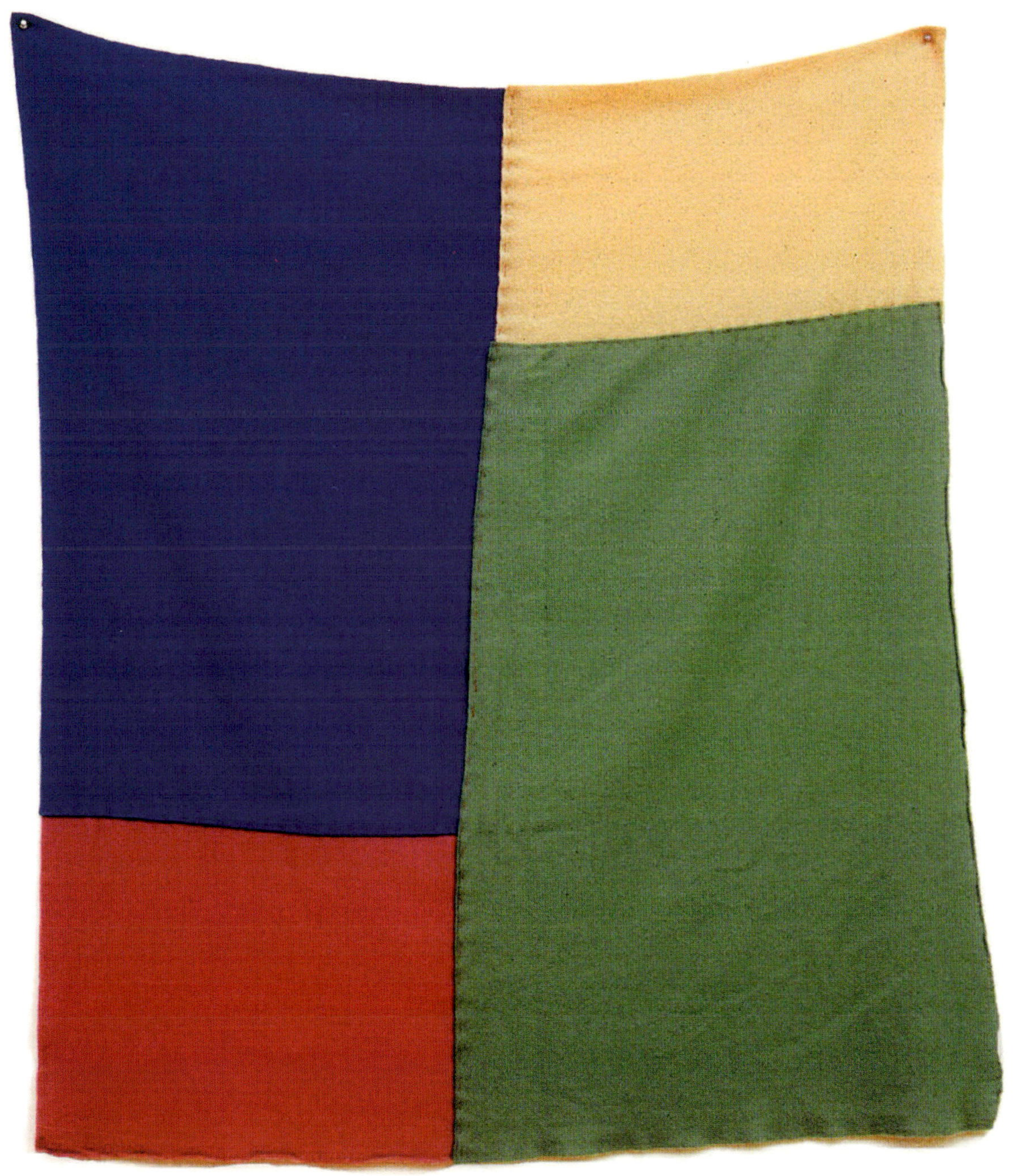

CATALOGUE OF WORKS

Matt Arbuckle

(all works Courtesy the artist)

1 *No Title*, 2013-2016, mixed media on found paper, eight pieces, 30 x 21 cm each.

2 *In Between*, 2016, acrylic on found paper, diptych, 102.5 x 72 cm.

3 *Seeing and Reading*, 2016, oil on board, 60 x 40 cm.

4 *Sliding Door Opportunity,* 2016, mixed media collage on found paper, polyptych, 86 x 55 cm.

Peter Atkins

(all works Courtesy the artist and Tolarno Gallery, Melbourne)

5 *Brunswick Journal,* 2005, mixed media, 20 pieces, 30 x 30 cm each.

6 *Louis Armstrong's Greatest Hits,* 2013, acrylic on tarpaulin, 215 x 205 cm.

7 *Miles Davis – Kind of Blue*, 2013, acrylic on tarpaulin, 215 x 205 cm.

8 *The Bix Beiderbecke Legend*, 2013, acrylic on tarpaulin, 215 x 205 cm.

9 *EP Project*, 2015-2016, mixed media, 18 pieces, 17.8 x 17.8 cm each.

Chris Carmody

(all works Courtesy the artist unless noted)

10 *Inner North*, 2013, sunlight on window-sheet, 140 x 122 cm.

11 *779.973 KER:KER*, 2015, acrylic on canvas, 70.5 x 66 cm. James and Jacqui Erskine Collection.

12 *WQ305.23 S3*, 2016, acrylic on canvas, 161.5 x 138.5 cm. Collection: Louis Carroll.

13 *001.42 L1*, 2016, acrylic on canvas, 163 x 103.5 cm.

14 *State 150 TOD*, 2016, acrylic on canvas, 120 x 80 cm.

15 *321.020943 RYD*, 2016, acrylic on canvas, 125 x 86 cm.

16 *Back of a Painting*, 2016, acrylic on canvas board, 50.8 x 60.9 cm.

17 *803 ABR*, 2016, acrylic on canvas board, 25.4 x 35.6 cm.

18 *Yellow Box 1.1*, 2016, cardboard on cardboard, 34.4 x 25.3 cm.

19 *Yellow Box 1.2*, 2016, cardboard on cardboard, 30.6 x 29.4 cm.

20 *Process Control Patch (PCP 6.1 -6.6),* 2016, acrylic on balsa, 6 pieces, 3.9 x 5.8 cm.

Nicole Ellis

(all works Courtesy the artist)

21 *Old Linen (orange)*, 2014, cotton, linen, nylon, acrylic paint, backed on cotton, 149.5 x 107.5 cm.

22 *Time-Lapse 1*, 2016, acrylic paint on fabric, on canvas, 150 x 110 cm.

23 *Time-Lapse 2*, 2016, acrylic paint on fabric, on canvas, 150 x 110 cm.

24 *Time-Lapse 3*, 2016, acrylic paint on fabric, on canvas, 150 x 110 cm.

25 *Time-Lapse 4*, 2016, acrylic paint on fabric, on canvas, 150 x 110 cm.

26 *Time-Lapse 5*, 2016, acrylic paint on fabric, on canvas, 150 x 110 cm.

27 *Time-Lapse 6*, 2016, acrylic paint on fabric, on canvas, 150 x 110 cm.

28 *Time-Lapse 7*, 2016, acrylic paint on fabric, on canvas, 183 x 152.5 cm.

29 *Time-Lapse 8*, 2016, acrylic paint on fabric, on canvas, 183 x 152.5 cm.

30 *Time-Lapse 9*, 2016, acrylic paint on fabric, on canvas, 183 x 152.5 cm.

Erwin Fabian

(all works Courtesy the artist, Australian Galleries, Melbourne and Robin Gibson Gallery, Sydney)

31 *Paradigm,* 2008, steel, 99 x 53 x 43 cm.

32 *Exit*, 2008, steel, 50 x 25 x 19 cm.

33 *Bloom*, 2010, steel, 246 x 129 x 117 cm.

34 *Epigram*, 2015, steel, 116 x 68 x 60 cm.

Robert Motherwell

(all works Collection: National Gallery of Australia, Canberra)

35 *Harvest with orange stripe (from 'Summer light' series)*, 1973, lithograph, collage, 76.3 x 30.6 cm.

36 *Harvest with blue shadow (from 'Summer light' series)*, 1973, lithograph printed in two colours from two aluminium plates; lithographic collage in seven colours, 76.4 x 30.4 cm.

37 *Pauillac no. 4 (from 'Summer light' series)*, 1973, lithograph printed in blue ink from one aluminium plate; hand torn lithographic image printed in three colours; embossing, 76.2 x 30.6 cm.

38 *America – La France variations I (from 'America – La France variations' series)*, 1983, colour lithograph, collage, 118 x 80.8 cm.

39 *America – La France variations IV (from 'America – La France variations' series)*, 1983, colour lithograph, collage, 118.6 x 81.2 cm.

40 *America – La France variations IX (from 'America – La France variations' series)*, 1983, colour lithograph, collage, 102.4 x 78 cm.

41 *America – La France variations II [collage study] (from 'America – La France variations' series)*, 1984, colour lithograph, collage, 114.9 x 79 cm.

42 *America – La France variations IV (from 'America – La France variations' series)*, 1984, lithograph, collage, 118.1 x 81.5 cm.

Elizabeth Newman

(all works Courtesy the artist and Neon Parc, Melbourne, unless noted)

43 *Blanket Painting*, 2002, wool fabric, 130 x 100 cm.

44 *Untitled*, 2005, bonded wool, 220 x 120 cm. Cruthers Collection of Women's Art, The University of Western Australia.

45 *Untitled*, 2008, found object, 170 x 110 cm.

46 *Mother Love*, 2009, fabric, glue, 130 x 130 cm.

47 *Jazzy One*, 2009, fabric on linen, 110 x 85 cm.

48 *Immaterial space isn't necessarily ethically superior 1*, 2012, print, 29 x 22 cm.

49 *Immaterial space isn't necessarily ethically superior 2*, 2012, print, 29 x 22 cm.

50 *Untitled*, 2014, collage, 29.5 x 21.5 cm.

51 *Untitled*, 2014, collage, 25 x 26 cm.

52 *Untitled*, 2014, collage, 26.5 x 24 cm.

Trish Roan

(all works Courtesy the artist, unless noted)

53 *Star map* 2014, photograph, 37.5 x 50 cm. Australian National University Art Collection.

54 *Iris*, 2016, video loop.

55 *Field*, 2016, mixed media.

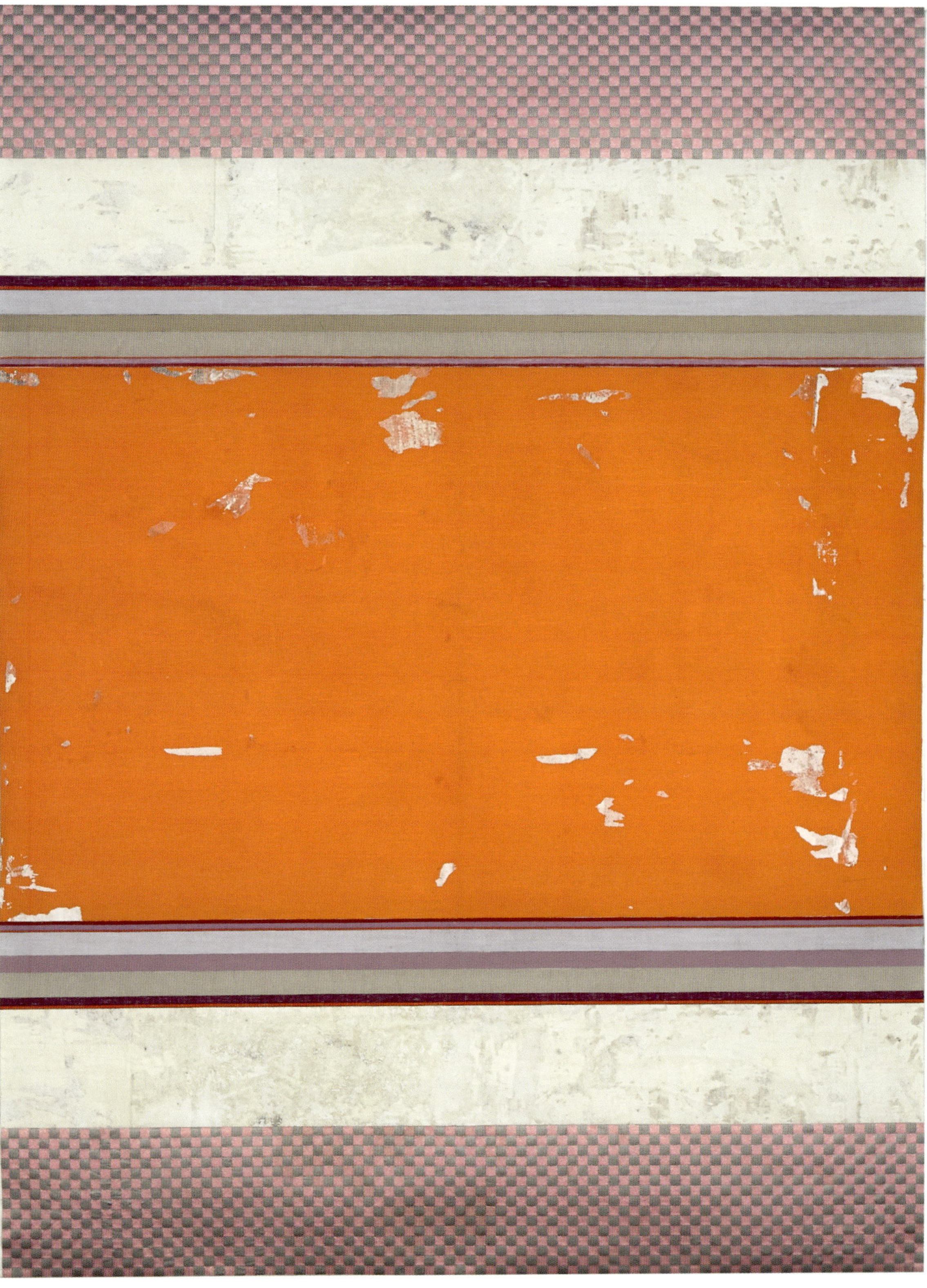

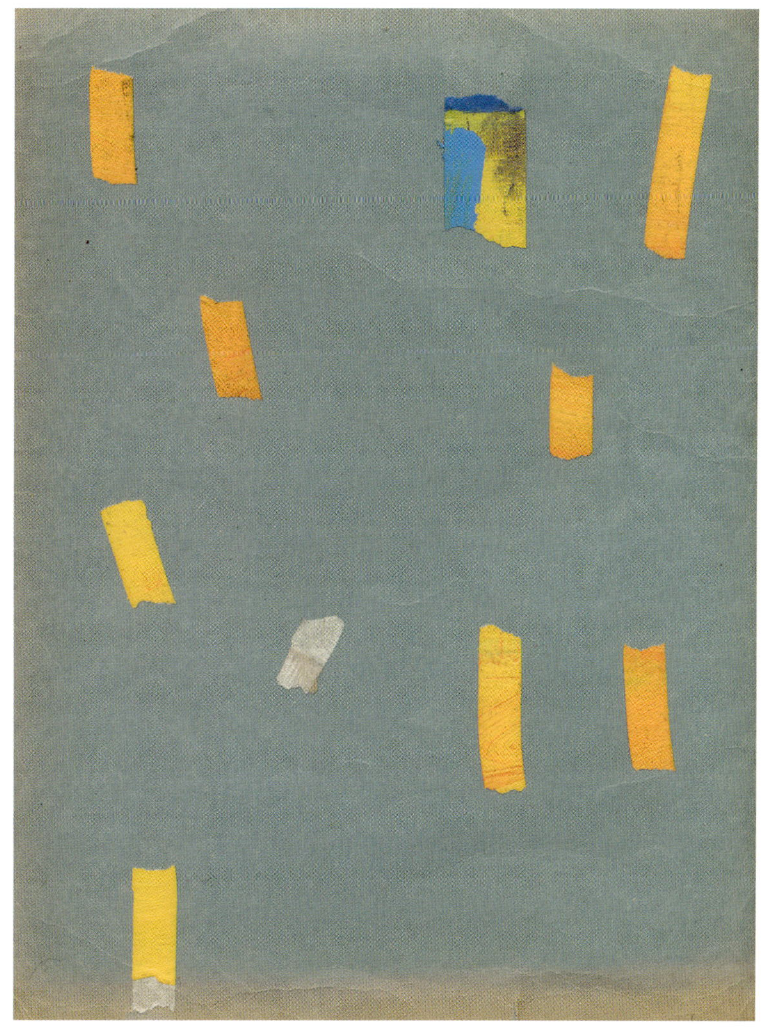

above: Matt Arbuckle, *No Title*, 2013-2016 (cat no 1);
opposite: Nicole Ellis, *Old Linen (orange)*, 2014 (cat no 21)

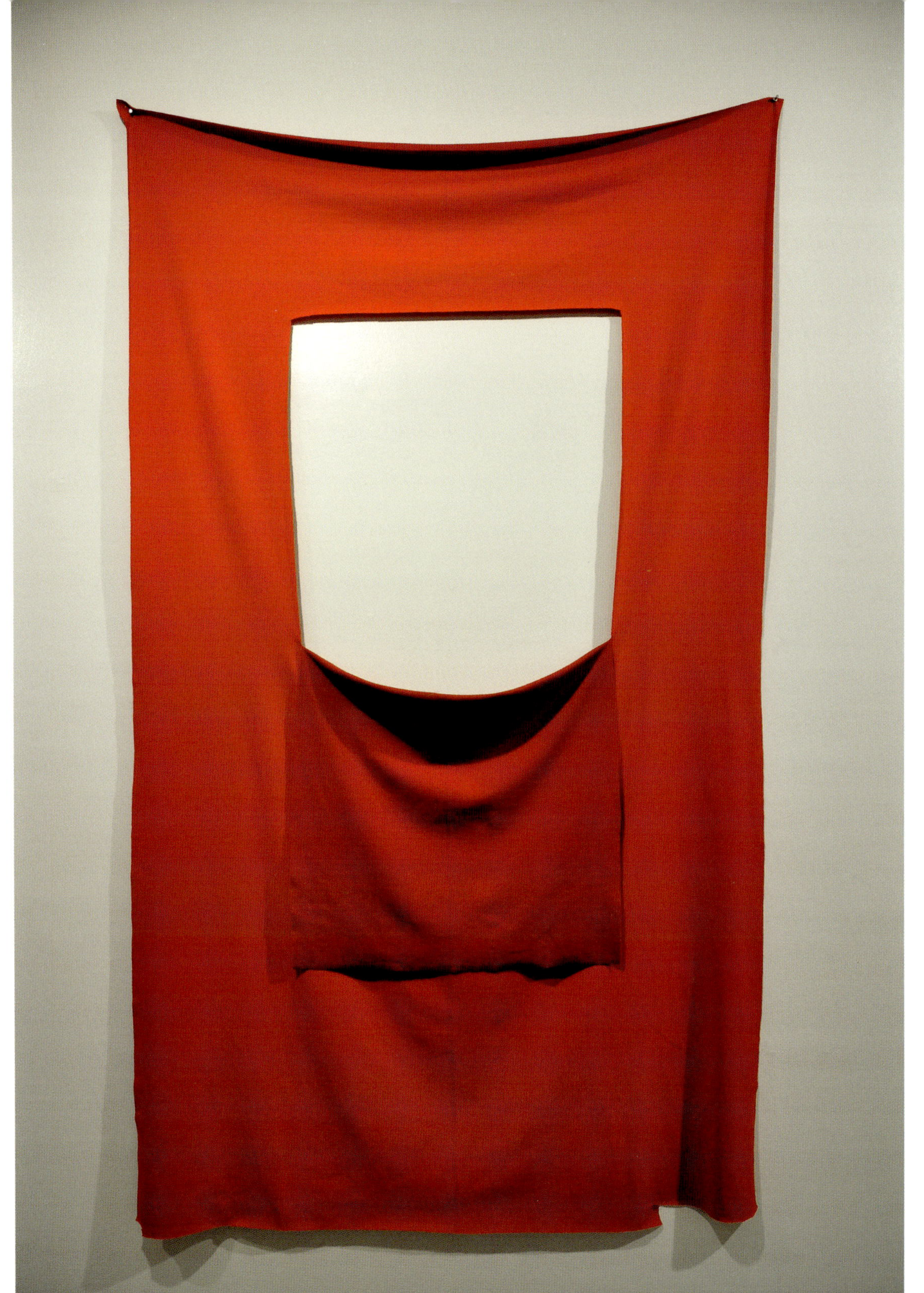

ACKNOWLEDGEMENTS

The curator would like to thank, first and foremost, the contributing artists – Matt Arbuckle, Peter Atkins, Chris Carmody, Nicole Ellis, Erwin Fabian, Robert Motherwell, Elizabeth Newman and Trish Roan – I am most grateful for their willingness to participate. Their discussions along the way helped immensely in shaping the exhibition. The Friends of the Drill Hall Gallery has been very supportive of this exhibition, making available special funding. I am grateful to those people who have help identify, locate and lend artworks for the exhibition. My particular thanks to Dr Jane Kinsman, Senior Curator, International Prints, Drawings and Illustrated Books, and Jacklyn Babington, Senior Curator, Contemporary Arts Practice, and the National Gallery of Australia for their assistance in the selection of Robert Motherwell's works; Gemma Weston, Curator, Cruthers Collection of Women's Art and Kate Hamersley at UWA Museums, the University of Western Australia; James and Jacqui Erskine; Louis Carrol; Emil Toonen; Adam Sims and Liverpool Street Gallery, Sydney; Geoff Newton and Neon Parc, Melbourne; Australian Galleries, Melbourne; Robin Gibson Gallery, Sydney; Tolarno Gallery, Melbourne. My thanks to Alec Hunter, Chloe Hobbs and the ANU New Music Ensemble, and also Shoeb Ahmad and hellosQuare for their musical response to collage. I am thankful for discussions with my colleagues at the Drill Hall Gallery and ANU Art Collection; to Terence Maloon for allowing me to run with this idea and for his exquisite editorial suggestions; my thanks to Jeanette Brand, David Boon, Anne Langridge, our install team: Joel Arthur, Zoe Brand, Joel Bliss, Chris Dalzell, Steve Harrison, Dioni Salas, and interns Clare Fealy and Yifang Cui. My greatest thanks to Kerryn, Perry and Miles.

Artist questionnaires and biographies are avaliable online: dhg.anu.edu.au

Elizabeth Newman, *Untitled*, 2005 (cat no 44)

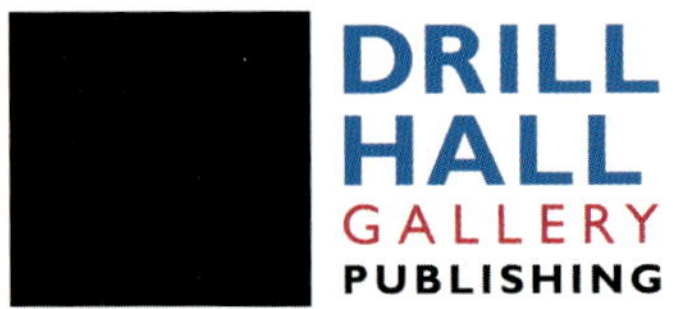

ISBN: 978-0-9954258-0-4
Published: November 2016
Text: Anthony Oates
Catalogue design: Anthony Oates
Photography: Matt Arbuckle, Peter Atkins, Sue Blackburn, Brenton McGeachie, National Gallery of Australia, Neon Parc, Elizabeth Newman, Viki Petherbridge, Trish Roan.
cover image: Nicole Ellis, *Time-Lapse* 7, 2016 (detail), acrylic paint on fabric on canvas, 183 x 152.5 cm. Courtesy the artist. Photo: Sue Blackburn.

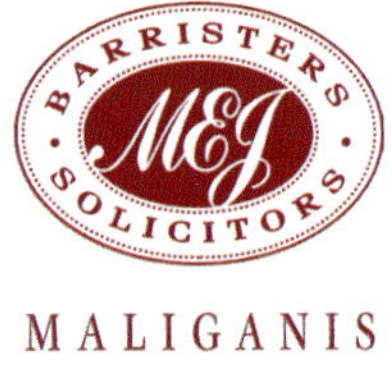

MALIGANIS
EDWARDS
JOHNSON

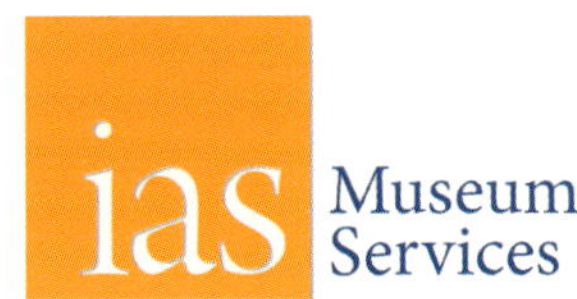

Director: Terence Maloon
Curator, Exhibitions: Tony Oates
Curator, Collection: David Boon
Manager, Outreach: Jeanette Brand
+ 61 2 6125 5832 dhg@anu.edu.au
dhg.anu.edu.au

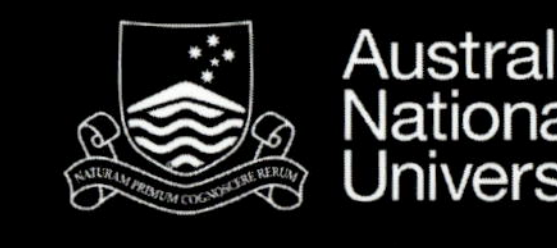

Australian
National
University